Highland Highways

Old Roads in Atholl

JOHN KERR FSA (Scot)

Foreword by His Grace the Duke of Atholl

JOHN DONALD PUBLISHERS LTD
EDINBURGH

ISBN 0 85976 245 9

British Library Cataloguing in Publication Data
Kerr, John
   Highland Highways: Old Roads in Atholl.
   1. Tayside (Scotland). Roads, history
   I. Title
   388.1094128

Phototypeset by Newtext Composition Ltd, Glasgow.
Printed & bound in Great Britain by Scotprint Ltd, Musselburgh.

Highland Highways

Foreword

For anyone interested in early communications in the Highlands of Scotland, the publication of one of John Kerr's booklets is a major event. The research which goes into them is prodigious, and the final result is an accurate and highly readable publication. This major book (the first he has written) combines all his previous publications, with much more detail about life in the settlements and shielings, and will be welcomed by all historians as an addition to our knowledge of Highland roads since the 13th century. This should make the difficulties facing early road builders such as General Wade easier to understand.

However, this is considerably more than a history book: it also traces the derivations of the names of the farms and dwellings alongside the roads it covers, and some of these are truly fascinating. I am confident that anyone will enjoy reading this book, and will also find it useful as a work of reference.

Blair Castle

His Grace the Duke of Atholl.

v

Acknowledgements

My sincere thanks go to His Grace the Duke of Atholl who has given me free access to all parts of the estate and permitted me to research his family archives in the Charter Room where Mrs Jane Anderson, archivist, has been of great assistance. Without the late Mr Alec MacRae this book would not have been written and I am deeply indebted to him for passing on so much of his knowledge of the area and also for his constant encouragement. I am very grateful to Mr John Cameron, *Atholl Country Collection* for showing me his old photographs of the locality and some of these appear in the book. My grateful thanks go to the many people of Atholl who have helped me in the preparation of this book. As the list is a long one, space will only allow me to mention the stalkers, keepers, shepherds and farmers who have been very helpful in telling me about the lie of the land. Without them, my walking, already extensive, would have been greatly increased.

Over the years I have been indebted to Mr Ian Fraser, School of Scottish Studies, for the patience he has shown and the assistance he has given me in translating the many Gaelic place names along the routes of these roads. My very special thanks go to Mr Hugh Barron, secretary of the Gaelic Society of Inverness because it was he who first gave me the chance to read a paper about these Atholl roads in 1975.

I would like to thank the following for permission to reproduce illustrations: The Duke of Atholl, Blair Castle; The Royal Commission on the Ancient & Historical Monuments of Scotland; National Galleries of Scotland; Mr John Cameron, Atholl Country Collection; University of St Andrews; Clan Donnachaidh Museum; Perth Museum and Art Gallery.

Contents

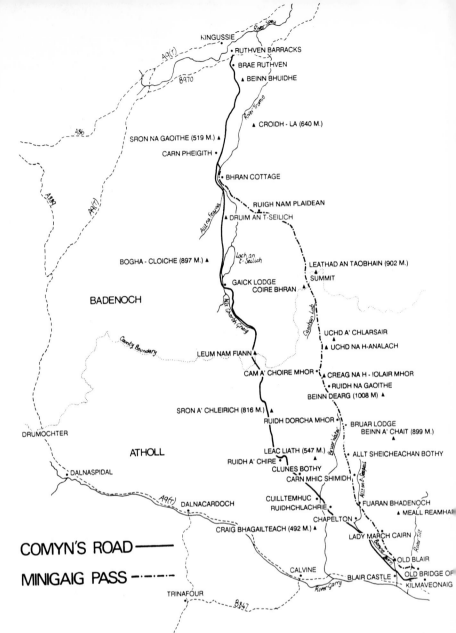

This map shows the different routes taken over the Grampian Mountains by Comyn's Road and the Minigaig Pass, both of which start in Blair Atholl and finish in Ruthven, yet take a different way across the mountains. The advantage that both these routes had over the Wade Road, forerunner to the A9, in achieving a saving of 15 to 16 miles is very apparent.

Introduction

A road is more than a line of communication linking two places. A road is an organic creation with a life of its own helping to support a way of life, a culture, along its entire length. Like people, each road is different and changes with the seasons, and, indeed, according to the time of day. Each road has its own characteristics, its own personality and its own story to tell.

Much has been written about the exploits and achievements of the great Highland road builders of the 18th and 19th centuries and the history of the construction of a network of roads in this mountainous area must start with General Wade. However, very little is known about Highland roads before this date. The word *road* hardly appears in documentation before the 16th century and although there are records of military and civil expeditions moving up and down the country, in no case were they described as using a highway. Before the construction of bridges which made definite routes for traffic, gradually forming into roads, expeditions seem to have been made across open country and travellers appeared to go as they pleased over the land, with little in the shape of a road to help them. Until the 16th century it was a belief that Scotland formed a distinct island, which lay on an east-west axis pointing towards Norway. In *La Popelinière Histoire de France* (1581), there is the expression *Les Catholiques des deux Isles*, the two islands being England and Scotland.

The publication of Mercator's Atlas at the end of the 17th century made people more acquainted with the geography of Scotland, but its remoteness and rough terrain created a natural barrier and travellers to the interior were few. Those who ventured forth preferred to keep to the east where the going was easier and some travelled by sea. Even at the close of the century Scotland was still regarded as a kind of Terra Incognita, a mystical country with strange and sometimes wild customs. Properly constructed roads seem to have been a development of the 17th century and it was not until the latter

1

part of that century that Highland roads appeared on maps. The first was called *A new map of Scotland, with the roads,* and was produced by Robert Greene in 1689. This shows a highway starting at Perth, passing through Atholl and crossing the Grampians by means of the Minigaig Pass, to reach the Moray Firth.

The parish of Blair Atholl lies equidistant between Edinburgh and Inverness. It became a united parish around 1650 when four smaller parishes, Struan, Kilmaveonaig, St Bride's in Old Blair and Kirkton of Lude in Glen Fender were merged to form one of the largest in the country. With the Perthshire/Inverness-shire watershed as its northern boundary and Tummelside to the south it is nearly 20 miles deep and up to 30 miles across at its widest part. The village of Old Blair, formerly Blair Town, was the core of a network of roads passing through the area. In the 13th century a road was built by the Red Comyn to link his castles in Blair and Ruthven in Badenoch and this was superseded in the 17th century by the route through the Grampians over the Minigaig Pass which later became a drove road. Both had the advantage of directness, being 16 miles shorter than the military road through Drumochter built by General Wade in the 18th century, which became the forerunner of the A9. A hundred years later the Parliamentary Commission for Highland Roads and Bridges extensively repaired and re-aligned the route and in the 1920s it was surfaced for the first time. A completely new highway through Atholl, which has only recently been completed, was built in the 1970/80s. Another important highway in the area ran to the north-east through Glen Tilt, to link Blair Atholl with Braemar in Aberdeenshire, and this was one of the few east-west routes in the Highlands. All these roads, which are no longer through routes, met at *Tigh Glas* the inn, which became an important centre till the early part of the 19th century and the advent of the road over the new Bridge of Tilt.

It was on the same road 30 years ago at another important 'filling station', the Blair Atholl garage, that I first met Mr Alec MacRae. Something he said sparked off a desire to learn more about this beautiful part of north Perthshire, and what began as a holiday interest has grown into a dedication. Up to now, five booklets are all that have been published about the deserted settlements and shielings and the people who lived in these remote glens. This book covers the problems they faced with the factor and indeed with each other, their hopes and fears, their struggle to survive in appalling conditions of climate and terrain and the effect of the roads on their lives.

I have translated many of the place names, as through them we get glimpses of a microcosm of life in this Highland parish. There is however a considerable variation in the spelling of these names because, from the 17th century, education was nearly always in English, and although Gaelic spelling is grammatically correct, the scribes spelt these names phonetically and I have therefore used the latest spellings in documents and maps, yet retained the original in quoted extracts. I have deliberately included many verbatim extracts from letters and reports because they provide a closer *feel* of conditions in these times. Whenever possible I have included grid references of places of interest along these roads even though many no longer exist, and these have come from sheets 35, 42 and 43 of the 1:50,000 series of Ordnance Survey maps.

The importance of the main way to the north across the centuries is shown by the fact that six of the eight chapters in this book are devoted to this subject. Space constraints do not allow me to use all the material available, yet even so, Wade and his military roads account for five chapters, in four of which we trace the actual route taken by this 18th century highway through Atholl. The split between the chapters is territorial rather than topographical with chapter 4 including Blair Castle grounds and environs while in chapter 5 we cross the Brae Lands of Faskally, Robertson land till 1767. The journey to Drumochter, through the 'Lochgarry' estate, is completed in chapter 6 and the strategic link to the south-west is covered in chapter 7. Finally in chapter 8 we look at the several roads in Glen Tilt and the narrative ends at the Perthshire/Aberdeenshire watershed.

Through *Highland Highways* I am attempting to show that before road building the Highlands was not the wild place it was assumed to be, divided by great mountain barriers and devoid of any means of communication, but a place populated by people with pride and purpose. I can only hope that those reading these pages may derive a little of the pleasure which years of research have given to me and that the picture I have tried to show may help to preserve for the future a reflection of what was once a vivid and vital part of Scotland's great heritage.

John Kerr

CHAPTER 1

Comyn's Road

The Grampian Mountain range linking the Garry with the Spey was one of the great natural barriers a traveller had to cross when venturing through the interior of the Highlands. Though not craggy and rugged like the Cairngorms and Cuillins, they must have presented a formidable obstacle to those early travellers. To a lesser extent this barrier still exists today in dividing the people of Atholl from those of Badenoch, the former gravitating towards Perth while the latter look to Inverness. Yet there has been a road through the Grampians since the 13th century – Comyn's Road. The Comyns were a proud Norman family who came over with William the Conqueror and at that time were Lords of Badenoch. It was while Henry, Earl of Atholl was away on the Crusades that the Red Comyn seized his opportunity, invaded Atholl and built Blair Castle, the oldest part of which is still Comyn's Tower. At this time the Red Comyn owned Ruthven Castle near Kingussie, thereby controlling the northern end of the passes over the Grampians, and by building the first recorded castle at Blair Atholl in 1269 he effectively controlled the southern end of these passes also and maintained a stranglehold on the entire area.

Tradition claims that the Red Comyn and his wife were passing through Atholl and, on arrival at the village of Kilmaveonaig on the east bank of the River Tilt, went to the inn for refreshments. They ordered some beer (in those days the chief drink of the Highlands) and were so taken by the quality of the ale that they asked the landlord where the ingredients came from. He told them the malt came from Perth, but it was the water from Aldnehearlain, a small stream running through the village, which gave his beer its special taste and flavour. There and then Comyn decided to transport the beer to his other castle at Ruthven and, after surveying the ground, built a road over the pathless tract of wilderness between his two castles. Whether the story of Comyn's desire for Atholl ale led directly to the building of the road bearing his name is accurate or not, we do not know. What is certain is that a highway, known as *Rathad nan Cuimeinach* (Comyn's Road), existed between Blair Atholl and Ruthven. An early manuscript tells us: 'There is a way from the gate of Blair in Atholl to Ruffen in Badenoch. Maid be David Comyn Earle of Atholl for carts to pass with wyne and the way is called Rad na Pheny or Way of Wane Wheills. It is laid with calsay in sundrie parts'.

Notable expeditions used this route. In 1295 King Edward I invaded Scotland at the head of an army of 30,000 foot and 5,000 heavily armed horse soldiers and, after successful campaigns in the Lowlands, led his army up the east coast to Montrose. From there he sent parties to survey the country of Badenoch and it seems likely the route they chose would have taken them along Comyn's Road as this was the only way of approaching Badenoch from the south. In 1500 a contract was drawn up between George, Earl of Huntly and John, 1st Earl of Atholl by which the inhabitants of Badenoch were permitted to pass through Atholl. The contract gave 'freedom for all and sundry of inhabitants of Badenoch to come and go through the said lands of Atholl with your goods and carriage, passing and repassing as often as you want. No one is to be stopped'. The existence of what appears to be an early example of a Right of Way through the Grampians in the 15th century indicates the presence of a well-defined route, Comyn's Road, almost certainly the oldest road in the Highlands to cross a mountain range.

The advantage of Comyn's Road over the modern way is distance. From Blair Atholl to Ruthven through Drumochter is 42 miles, while the same journey can be achieved using Comyn's Road in 27 miles, a saving of 15 miles. The much shorter distance would have been an important factor when travelling on foot or horseback. Admittedly Comyn's route would be impassable in winter as it climbs to a height well over 1,000 feet higher than Drumochter, but this was of little consequence in those days as there was a minimum of travel during these months anyway.

Comyn's Road starts at *Kilmaveonaig* (Church of St. Beoghna) 879 657 where all that remains of the village where he

The bothy at Clunes on Comyn's Road which is now an Estate track. The Kirrachan Shielings are situated over the ridge and Comyn's Road reaches its highest point of almost 2,600 feet as it crosses Sron a' Chleirich, the prominent hill in the background.

reputedly tasted the local brew is a small Episcopalian chapel of Celtic origin. St. Beoghna, who died circa 606, was second Abbot of Bangor. The actual route for the first two miles is largely circumstantial because forestry, cultivation over 700 years and a multitude of paths and tracks have obscured the original route. However there is only one place where it could have crossed the River Tilt and that is by the Priest's Ford near the croy which is the start of the lade for the Mill of Blair. At this point the river is at its shallowest and would make a good crossing point to the west bank and America Park, location of the present-day caravan site. When this was ploughed up as part of the 'Dig for Victory' campaign in the Second World War, no trace of an old road was found, indicating that the route must have been to the south of the Park, to join what is now the main castle drive. This was a much older grass track known as Gregor's Walk.

From here the road would have passed in front of the castle and crossed the Banvie Burn near *Diana's Grove*. This was laid out in 1737 and four years later the lead statue of Diana with a deer was purchased for £22 and also statues of Apollo and

Comyn's Road is seen from the air coming in from the right to cross the steep ravine formed by Allt a' Mhuilinn, by means of a ford. A maze of peat haggs and bogs is visible at the source of the stream.

Ceres. In 1751 a circular summer-house called the *Temple of Fame* was built, in which small plaster busts were placed. It fell down in 1864 and was not rebuilt. Richard Pococke describes the scene in 1760: 'This stream (Banvie) passes through a vale which is most beautifully planted with many sorts of American trees. This is called Diana's Grove, from a statue of her and a stag on rising ground from which there are eight walks.'

After climbing gently across open land, the road enters the Whim Plantation at an old gateway. The Whim, built in 1762 was described by the Hon. Sarah Murray on her tour of Scotland in 1796 as 'a sham castle, backed by thick woods'. When the Duke told the Rev. Stewart he was at a loss as to what to call it, the minister said it would be difficult to name as it was just a 'whim'. At this point the track is clear as it winds its way through the trees, to arrive at a point above the *Quarry Bridge* 853 677 which spans the Banvie. This bridge was named after an old quarry a few yards upstream and was built in 1770, eight years later than the Rumbling Bridge, a mile downstream. This is a fine stone bridge which bears witness to the fact that the Banvie, in times of spate, can actually 'rumble' the stones and rocks in its bed. As the track clears the trees the landscape changes dramatically and the road can be seen boldly picking its way across the empty moorland a few hundred yards higher up than the Duke's Nine Mile Drive. Here it passes through a dyke, important as a means of establishing the antiquity of the road. Many of these dykes were built around 1770 from money loaned by the Duke at 7½% interest, to enclose the land. Where the road meets the dyke there is no gateway, indicating that by the 18th century it had long since fallen into disuse. A series of zigzags on the hillside opposite indicate an old path once used by peat cutters, fetching their peat from *Tom nan Cruach* (hillock of peat stacks). Peat for the castle fires would have been cut and stacked here to dry before being barrowed down the track. One can still see footings of several stone enclosures built to protect the freshly cut peats from damage by stags.

The track continues to rise gently and joins the Nine Mile Drive to the source of the Banvie. An extensive settlement lies on the south-facing slope of Meall Dubh, where large areas of ground have been cleared on the west and east sides leaving a rough, stony strip in between. This is called *Chapelton* 839 696 where the remains of five shieling bothies, which probably formed the original settlement, have been found near the river. In 1713 a three-year lease was granted to Lauchlan McIntosh for the shieling of Riechapel, but as pressure for space in the valley grew, tenants started settling in the foothills and Chapelton became a permanent settlement. The remains of at least 14 buildings can be seen, with two kilns and associated enclosures. In *Roy's Military Survey* of 1747-55 it is clearly marked 'chapel' though no trace of a place of worship has been found. On a cold dark night in 1723 disaster struck Donald Stewart, one of the tenants. He was described as coming from 'honest parents – a married man free of all public scandal or church censure having behaved honestly and civilly'. He 'had his barn and all his corn and most part of his bed clothes lying in that large barn burnt up quite by accidental fire in the dead time of the night, carried thither by the violence of the wind on Wednesday night, sixth of this month (November) by which loss he is rendered a great object of pity and charity of tender hearted Christians'. Within a few days the estate had allowed

Comyn's Road descending from near the summit of Sron a' Chleirich
to the ford at Allt a' Mhuilinn. This is the best preserved part of the
road throughout its 27 miles.

him £12 Scots off his rent. The parochial register shows that at
least six families lived here throughout the 18th century and it
was still inhabited around 1860.

Bruar

At the head of the glen the Nine Mile Drive sweeps southwards
but Comyn's Road heads north-west, descending to Glen Bruar
and reaches *Ruidhchlachrie* (stony shieling) 819 706, which
initially was a shieling and was leased to Robertson of
Auchleeks in 1687 for a rental of £20 Scots and two wedders,
value £4. By 1723 the lease was granted to Gregor Murray, the
miller at Blair, who was paying £50 sterling and 'two good and
sufficient hill swine, twelve capons and four bolls of meal,
mortified by the late Marquis of Atholl to poor old decayed
tenants of the parish of Blair Atholl'. There is evidence of a
number of families living here in the 18th century and the
remaining house is in good condition and still roofed. This was
built in 1813 when William Robertson transported lime and
wood at a cost of £9.0.0. while Peter Grant charged £14.10.2

for mason work and J. Jack carried out the slating work at a cost of £3.12.7. Ruidhchlachrie was described as a good croft capable of taking at least 30 sheep and some cows and was deserted in 1939 when the last inhabitant departed to fight in the war and although he returned to the area, he never came back to his croft.

It is a short distance from here to the *Bruar* (bridge stream), along a well-defined track and the river is crossed by a ford marked on the first edition of the 6 inch Ordnance Survey map. Nowadays there is no need for a ford as much of the water is diverted for a hydro scheme and the Bruar at this point is a pale shadow of its former splendour. Once across, Comyn's Road passes near to another settlement called *Cuilltemhuc* (pig's nook) 816 713, where a single-storey slated house stands. Its lease was due to expire in 1795 and as the tenant had indicated his intentions to relinquish it, the estate made plans to advertise it through a public notice at all the neighbouring parish churches. At the time its rent was 16 guineas a year and the highest offer received was 10 guineas. Eventually it was disposed of for 13 guineas a year. Living here over a hundred years ago was my favourite character, the laughing man of Cuilltemhuc, who was found blind drunk in a water trough and laughing his head off. No one has ever discovered the subject of his merriment, whisky excepted!

Beyond Cuilltemhuc, the road is difficult to find as it winds its way up a gradual slope avoiding bogs and streamlets to reach the bothy at *Clunes*. This stands on a bend in the estate track which we leave after a mile to reach *Ruidh a' Chire* (shieling of the combs) 793 737, often referred to as the Kirrachan Shielings. It is located at the junction of two rivers and the remains of twelve bothies can be seen in a wide area of pasture. The Kirrachans were feued as pasture to two other estates, Shierglas and Strathgarry, both located south of the Garry and about eight miles distant.

Since 1665 the Shierglas tenants had been astricted to the Mill of Blair: 'Tenants shall come with their grindable Cornes to the Miln of Blair to grind the samen and pay therefore the knaveships and services allenarlie but only multures'. In return in 1727 they were granted 'perpetual servitude of pasturage' over half the Kirrachans, 'with full power to sheal and pasture

Gaick Lodge, where the powers of evil and the supernatural were unequalled anywhere in the Highlands, stands in a desolate, windswept glen with mountains on each side towering to a height of nearly 3,000 feet. Loch an t-Seilich, the largest of the three Gaick lochs is visible in the top left-hand corner.

their bestial yearly'. By 1800 there was only one bothy still standing in the shieling and this had been rebuilt with windows and roofed to form a small shooting house. By 1830 the Duke had purchased the feu rights from both Strathgarry and Shierglas estates for £900 each.

The Statistical Account of 1792 describes a shieling in Atholl in the following way: 'Lower down is heath, peat-bog, valleys full of pretty good pasture, and here and there a green spot, with huts upon them; to which the women, children, and herds, retire with the cattle for the summer season.' The system of transhumance began when arable agriculture started, as stock had to be removed to a safe distance from cultivation itself. Shielings were found wherever climate or topography caused a seasonal variation in the value or availability of pasture so that man and his flocks must move their base at least twice in the course of a year to win maximum use from the land. Only when the terrain was fit enough for nothing but pasture – at least for part of the year – and was quite incapable of conversion to arable land, would a shieling system persist. Such conditions were to be found in Scotland where high latitude brought cool conditions. Out-pastures were occupied by cattle and other stock during the summer months and the grazing grounds and bothies for the herdsmen and dairymaids were known as shielings.

There is no trace of the road till it reaches the long ridge of *Sron a' Chleirich* (promontory of the cleric) 784 769, where it is easy to pick up on firm ground. It passes within a short distance of the summit marked with a trig point, and here it reaches its highest point, almost 2,600 feet. The other side of the mountain is much steeper, the sharp gradient being shaped by *Allt a' Mhuilinn* (mill stream), which has formed a ravine – a major obstacle to any road builder, especially in the 13th century. The terrain higher up however is even worse, where the source of the stream is formed from a maze of bogs and peat haggs, making the route in this direction impossible. There is one place where a road could cross *Allt a' Mhuilinn* 781 773, a perfectly-formed ford with a firm base and wide enough to take carts. Located as it is between the ravine and peat bogs higher up, it provides the only place for crossing this stream. After descending to Feith na Mad, a stream which at one time was paved at the crossing, Comyn's Road is clearly visible as it climbs steeply to *Bac na Creige* (bank of the rock) 775 797 and the march between Atholl and Badenoch, marked by the remains of a rusty fence. Here it has the directness of a Roman road as it continues into Badenoch across firm and flat ground. It was here that the Scottish Horse held army manoeuvres for four days in 1907 and stationed two scouts on bicycles in Comyn's Pass.

Fingal's Leap

Nearby there is *Leum nam Fiann* (Fingal's leap) 773 805 and this is where Lord Walter Comyn of Ruthven met his terrible end. In a mood of cruel sensuality, Walter decreed that all the women of Badenoch between the ages of 12 and 30 years should work naked in the fields and he was returning from Atholl to ensure his wicked deeds were being carried out when retribution caught up with him here. As the manuscript says: 'He ended miserablie being torn in pieces with a hors in Badenoch whair, falling from his hors, his fute stak in the stirrop was brocht to Blair by the said hors'. It appears the horse was found, foaming at the mouth with no rider on its back, but dragging one of Walter's legs from the stirrup at a place up Glen Tilt called *Leth-Chois* meaning one foot. A search was promptly made and his body was discovered beside the road with two eagles preying on it. Comyn's gory end was attributed to witchcraft and the eagles were reckoned to represent two of the mothers of the harvest girls. It is a desolate, awesome spot and a centuries-old Badenoch curse, *Diol Bhaltair an Gaig Ort* (Walter's fate of Gaick on you) recalls his terrible ending.

An isolated bothy ruin lies just off the road. This was used by elderly stalkers who would be positioned here to observe the movements of deer and to prevent the herds from straying across the march into Atholl. From here the road descends steeply by means of a series of sharp bends till it reaches *Allt Gharbh Ghaig,* (rough stream of Gaick) 775 818 where the crossing is achieved by means of a ford often impassable in times of spate. The hillside opposite is called *Toman Caorinn* (the rowan slope) 775 825. This beautiful tree is a native of the Highlands and its wood was once used by wheelwrights and coopers, but it is probably best known as a protection against witchcraft as the highlander believed that any part of it would ward off evil. The dairymaid when driving her cattle to the shieling would carefully lay a rod of rowan over the door of the bothy at night, and on May 1st would make her sheep and lambs pass through a hoop. In some parts berries were eaten when ripe and a strong spirit, not an evil one, was distilled!

Gaick

Comyn's Road appears to follow the existing track on the valley floor as it opens out to reveal *Gaick Lodge* (cleft) 757 849. Gaick has had an evil reputation unequalled anywhere in the Highlands. Nowhere has the power of the supernatural been so evocative and nowhere else has there been such a series of fatalities. Many are the tales of misdeed and misfortune in the steep confines of this glen and a Gaelic bard of the 18th century once penned these words of warning: 'Black Gaick of the wind – whistling crooked glens, ever enticing her admirers to destruction'. This feeling of evil and fear was in existence long before the disaster which overwhelmed the Black Officer and his four stalwart companions in 1799 and which is commemorated by a memorial stone. It marks the spot where the old Lodge was situated when it was destroyed by an avalanche on New Year's Eve 1799, killing all the inhabitants including the Black Officer, Captain MacPherson of Ballachroan. Several days later the Lodge was found to be destroyed, torn to shreds by some powerful malevolent force. Captain MacPherson was the army recruiting officer of the district and consequently was feared by the local people, many believing he was in league with the devil. The annihilation, so sudden and complete was put down to supernatural causes.

The Loss of Gaick
There's a voice on the gale and a shriek on the blast;
Rude rages the tempest, the snow falleth fast;
The corpse lights are flickering over the heath –
Foreboding of woe, the omens of death.
Brow-wrinkled, sage-eld, with fear seems opprest,
And the mother more close clasps the bab to her breast,
For the sights and sounds of that terrible night
Struck the hearts of the boldest with deadly affright;
They deemed, from the signs upon earth and in air,
That the fiend from the spit rout and revel held there.
Upon that night so wild and rude,
In Gaick's stern sombrous solitude,
A haunted scene of weird look gloom,
Where fierce Lord Walter dreed his doom,
A band of gallant men convene,
The shealing, from the blast, their screen.

The famous avalanche is reputed to occur every 100 years and it happened again in 1911 missing Gaick Lodge by a few yards. Lord Selkirk's Well is situated a quarter-mile south of the Lodge and 'applies to an excellent spring of water issuing out of the rock'. A little to the north there is the Duke of Gordon's Well, which he considered the best water in Gaick. It is worth recording here that this is the only place-name that indicates the long association of that family with the district. *Loch an t-Seilich* 757 865, the largest of the Gaick lochs, lies north of the Lodge and means willow loch. The willow was put to endless use, the bark being employed in tanning leather and the foliage was an acceptable food for cattle and horses. Young twigs were used in basket-work and even for making rope.

> There is a high wind on the Willoch Loch,
> There's another wind on the Loch of the Dune.
> I will reach the Loch of Brottin
> Ere sleep comes upon my eye.

Comyn's Road runs to the west of the loch and here it is easy to find as it is now used as a pony track. After a mile it climbs quickly up the shoulder of Boghacloiche and then down a long gentle slope to *Glen Tromie* (glen of the elder), once described by an old Gaelic bard as '*Gleann Tromaidh nan Siantan* (Glen Tromie of the stormy blasts). Next we cross *Allt na Fearna* (alder burn) and like the willow, the alder was used extensively. It was known as Scotch mahogany because of its colour and was made into furniture. When boiled, the leaves would provide a remedy for burns and inflammation and when fresh leaves were laid on swellings they were said to soothe. Often highlanders would place fresh alder leaves on the soles of their feet, when fatigued after a long journey.

Within half a mile, the Minigaig Road fords the Tromie and joins Comyn's Road for the final five miles to Ruthven. *Cnoc a' Cheannaiche* (pedlar's knoll) is nearby. This knoll was where a travelling merchant would take up his position on an appointed day to exchange and barter his goods and wares and the remains of a solitary bothy bear witness to his bartering. As the road climbes out of the glen it passes a prominent cairn, *Carn Pheigith* (Peggy's Cairn) 775 934. Who Peggy was is lost in the mists of time, but it is believed to relate to a suicide in the 14th century. A strange custom prevailed that when anyone took their own life, the body would be buried on the march between two lairds, thus confusing the spirit which would not know which way to go. Heaps of stones were erected over the graves of the dead to secure them from wolves and it became customary to toss another stone on top as you passed, hence the proverb, 'were I dead you would not throw a stone on it', meaning – you don't have much friendship for me.

Ruthven

Comyn's Road crosses open country for a couple of miles, skirts the western slope of *Beinn Bhuidhe* (yellow hill) and reaches

Perched on an ancient man-made mound, Ruthven Barracks, formerly a seat of the Comyns, has commanding views across the Spey and marks the end of the road.

Brae Ruthven (red place) 762 989, in 1880 a settlement containing several crofters' dwellings, thatched and in good order. Now it only consists of a byre. In 1727 John McLawrence and James Robertson of Brae Ruthven were admonished for being drunk on the Lord's Day as on their way there after attending divine service, they were seen struggling with one another. Also, and more serious, McLawrence was observed carrying creels on his back. The Kingussie Kirk Session found that both had breached the Sabbath and both had to stand before the next Congregation and be severely rebuked.

From here it is a short distance to our destination, Ruthven Barracks, and on the way we pass a small area of rough ground in a field. Marked as a graveyard it is probably the place where the dead of the garrison were buried. *Ruthven Barracks* 765 997 were reconstructed by General Wade for his dragoons on the site of the 13th century castle built by Comyn. This was described in a letter by Timothy Pont as 'The only and principal dwelling of the Lord of the Country, well seated upon a green bank about a bow shot from the river'. The barracks were only to stand for some 25 years before being burnt down in 1746 on the orders from Bonnie Prince Charlie after Culloden. The village of Ruthven, being the castle town of Badenoch is a place of great antiquity and in former times it had a courthouse, jail, mill, shop and school. The Comyns left a reputation in Badenoch for rapacity and cruelty and their treachery has passed into a proverb:

Fhad bhitheas craobh 'sa choill
Bithidh foill 'sna Cuiminich.
Meaning:
While in the wood there is a tree
A Comyn will deceitful be.

CHAPTER 2

The Minigaig Pass

At some period before the 17th century, Comyn's Road was replaced by the route through the Minigaig Pass as the main way across the Grampians. One reason for Comyn's Road falling into disuse was that the Minigaig route was nearly two miles shorter. Another could be that whereas Comyn's Road embraced two heights at Sron a' Chleirich and the County March, the Minigaig route had only one which was at the watershed. An early traveller of this route was the Marquis of Montrose who returned to Scotland in 1644 and with an army sought to free the nation from the oppressive influence of the three Scottish magnates, Hamilton, Huntly and Argyll. Hard-pressed by Argyll, he withdrew his army into the wilds of Badenoch where he knew the enemy's main strength, their cavalry, would be useless. Being anxious for the men of Atholl to join him, he marched to Atholl with such speed that in one night in November he covered 24 miles across a wild, desolate and snow-clad track and that route took him through the Minigaig Pass.

Early Maps

A 1721 manuscript states: 'The journey from Ruthven to Blair Atholl by crossing the Minigaig was a distance of 24 miles but there was another way to the South over Drumochter which was six miles longer'. The fact that Minigaig was used in preference to Drumochter shows the importance of the former route and emphasises that it was the main way through the Grampians before the military road. This is borne out when one studies early maps of the Highlands. The first map to show a road through the Grampians was produced by Robert Greene in 1689. It was called *A new map of Scotland, with the roads* and shows the route between Blair Atholl and Ruthven in a straight line. This was followed in 1718 by Herman Moll's *A Pocket Companion of Roads in the North Part of Great Britain called Scotland* and once again there was a direct way between the two

19

Herman Moll's pre-military road map of northern Perthshire produced in 1725, shows the Minigaig Pass route taking the direct line from Blair Atholl to Ruthven by passing through Glen Bruar. There is no sign of the Wade Road across Drumochter since it was not built for another four years.

places. In a more detailed map by Moll, called *North part of Perthshire, containing Atholl and Broadalbin* produced in 1725, the route can be seen running up the east bank of the Bruar in a direct north-westerly line to Ruthven, crossing the Minigaig Mountains. My final pre-military road map was again produced by Moll in 1725 and shows the roads between *Innersnait, Ruthven of Badenoch, Kiliwhiman and Fort William*. In it, the main route to the north runs in a direct line, passing over the *Moor of Minigog*. In all these maps there is no trace of a road over the Drumochter Pass proving that before the military road was completed in 1729, the main way across the Grampians was through the Minigaig Pass.

By 1745 maps of the King's Roads were appearing, showing the Minigaig route in the same style as the recently completed network of military roads. According to legend, a company of soldiers perished in a savage storm when marching over the Minigaig, north to Ruthven in the same year. The *Scots Magazine*, reporting the '45 in some detail, tells us that parties of troops were sent to scour the Minigaig Hills where some rebels were lurking and on 19th May, Brigadier Mordaunt with the Royal Pultney's and Semphill's Battalions and six pieces of cannon arrived at Perth, having travelled from Inverness by the hill road, meeting no disturbance during their march. Although this indicates that the Minigaig was still in reasonable repair, its decline as a main thoroughfare had started. Other maps produced at the same time described it as 'Summer Road to Ruthven' or 'Summer Road' or even 'Old Road from Blair to Ruthven'. James Stobie's 1780 map shows it as 'Foot Road from Strathspey to Blair' and its decline was complete. It still continued to be used however, by local people travelling between Blair Atholl and Ruthven as instanced by this letter from the Duke of Gordon to the Duke of Atholl in 1797:

'I had a very pleasant ride through your Forest of Bruar and saw a great many deer in my way to Minigaig. I was lucky in having good weather till I got in sight of Pitmean otherwise I should not have much pleasure in the journey, as the roads are not what they call 'weel dighted' in Aberdeenshire, particularly at the pass of Uchd na h-analach which by the favour of the moon I got very well over.'

(Uchd na h-Analach is the steep ridge at the head of Glen Bruar).

Cattle Drovers

At the start of the 19th century the Mingaig route down Glen Bruar became an important artery for furtive communication by cattle drovers who by this means could avoid the three tolls on the military road at the County March, Edendon and Bruar. John McGregor, County March tollman in 1829 stated that at least 300 cattle and some horses were coming that way and the drover was advising others to follow. 'These animals would lie all night in the deer forest, unless prevented', he said. 'As this is injurious to the toll men and also the forest, I though it my duty to mention it'. In September of the same year the Blair overseer reported that in three days he had counted 24 fillies and 592 cattle passing through Glen Bruar to the south. Later he challenged drovers with 13 fillies and 102 head of cattle but they would not agree to come by the military road. Memoranda at the time show the concern this caused the Atholl estate. One stated: 'There should be no difficulty in stopping them and the Minigaig could easily be closed to drovers. If a few were charged half a merk each for trespassing, they would soon find another route. No drove can claim the right either of driving through a hill such as Minigaig or to lie on the grass for the night.' However Atholl foresters were assisting the drovers by selling them whisky which was 'liberally' paid for, and if not, presents were given to the forester's wife and children. Commenting on all this, the factor maintained that when challenged six years earlier, drovers refused to turn back saying they were entitled to use the route as it was a public road. He also stated that since a new forester had been installed in Bruar Lodge, no whisky had been sold to drovers. The Minigaig continued to be used by drovers until the start of the 20th century.

The origin of the name Minigaig is obscure, Dr Watson in his *History of the Celtic Place Names of Scotland,* saying it comes from Mion Gag meaning 'mount of little cleft'. This explanation is not entirely satisfactory because from a geographical viewpoint there is no cleft on the pass. The pass is along the side of a hill and its characteristic feature is the extraordinary distance for which it remains level. There is a Gaelic word Min meaning level or smooth and this is more likely to be the meaning.

St. Bride's Church

The Minigaig route is shown in its entire length, with remarkable clarity in Roy's Survey produced in 1747-1755. Our journey starts at *St. Bride's Church* 866 665, in Old Blair, but there is strong evidence to suggest it continued in a southerly direction to Dunkeld and beyond. St. Bride's was featured in the Bagimond Rolls of the 13th century, paying tithes to Rome of four merks a year and was therefore an ancient parish of some importance. As well as being the principal church of the Atholl family, it contains the vault in which Viscount Dundee was buried. A tablet on the inner face of the south wall bears the following inscription: 'Within this vault beneath are interred the remains of John Graham of Claverhouse, Viscount of Dundee who fell at the battle of Killiecrankie 27 July 1689, aged 46. This memorial is placed here by John, 7th Duke of Atholl KT 1889'.

Daniel Defoe visited the area in 1769 and portrayed the church as a 'poor old Kirk, the pews all broken down, doors open, full of dirt where the minister preached once a week', while in 1811 it was depicted as a 'mean looking church, resembling an English barn'. Dorothy Wordsworth was kinder, saying it was the most interesting object she saw at Blair, shaded with trees. The church was surveyed in 1820 and although the walls were sound, the roof had entirely gone and the following year the Duke suggested that the churches of Blair and Struan, both of which were too small and in bad states of repair, should be closed and a new, larger church built in the centre of the parish, near the manse at Baluain. The scheme was opposed and St. Bride's completely rebuilt, yet, within three years, a decision was taken to build a new church on the Haugh of Blair, beside the recently made parliamentary road through the village, and St. Bride's fell into disuse again.

From the church the road passes along Minigaig Street in Old Blair and stays on the north side of the *Banvie* (pig stream), following a dyke which separates the Den Plantation from Glackley Park. After a gentle climb through a fir plantation it reaches open country. Here there are two tracks in the heather along the slope of *Meall Reamhar* (round hill). The upper of the two is a peat road and the Minigaig descends across the slope and just before reaching the West Hand estate road, passes beside *Lady March Cairn* 851 690. This stands over six feet in height and was built in the time of the 7th Duke who picnicked here with Lady March. She started a small cairn and workmen repairing the road nearby built a larger version. The road crosses *Allt Na Moine Baine* (stream of white moss) by means of a concrete culvert, replacing a fine stone arched bridge built in 1881 and demolished in the 1963 spate. In a mile, the Minigaig leaves the estate road near a perfectly shaped round well or spring called *Fuaran Bhadenoch* (well of Badenoch) 843 710, further proof that this road crossed the Grampians. The well is circular, 2 feet 6 inches in diameter and marked by a vertical stone slab.

The road is clearly visible as it traverses *Meall Dubh* (black hill) to reach *Carn Mhic Shimidh* (Lovat's cairn) 838 723, mostly destroyed by vandals in 1971. Once, when the Atholl men were away from the district, a band of Frasers seized the opportunity

St Bride's Church in Old Blair, pictured in 1860 with part of the west end still roofed following repairs in 1820. Within three years the main road was re-routed away from the village and again St Bride's fell into disuse.

to raid the country and on their return with their loot, one of the party asked the leader if he had sworn that he would leave no horses, cattle, sheep or even domestic fowls alive. If that was so, he had just heard a cock crow in a nearby farm (probably Chapelton). The leader agreed and promptly sent back a small party to destroy the offending cock. Meanwhile a number of Atholl men had raised the alarm and, encountering the party, murdered them all except one whom they kept hostage but afterwards killed when he tried to escape. A similar number of Atholl men then dressed in the dead mens' plaids and proceeded slowly to rejoin the main body of Frasers, waiting for them at the roadside. This gave time for a much larger body of Atholl men to go round by the Bruar and at a given signal, the Frasers were attacked simultaneously from the front and from behind and were soon overcome. The spot where this engagement took place is marked by the cairn, the leader of the Frasers being killed while calling for his horse.

The bothy and two stable stalls at *Allt Sheicheachan* (burn of the hides) 835 737 are situated at the end of the West Hand road, 5¾ miles from the castle. It was built in 1881 but earlier a shieling was situated upstream, first mentioned in a 1669 document as being leased to tenants of Blair Atholl. The way across the stream is marked by a ford and the road is clearly visible as is mounts *Druim Dubh* (black ridge), passing a cairn believed to commemorate a shepherd murdered over 300 years ago by marauding clans. Only 60 years ago a horse and cart could pass along this stretch of the road, travelling to Glen Bruar and the Lodge. *Glen Bruar* (bridge stream) was aptly described by William Scrope, the sporting tenant, at the beginning of the last century:

'About eight miles north of Blair Atholl, you descend into a glen which is wild and desolate. The heather, being old is rather of a brown than a purple colour but there is some relief of greensward near the Lodge and more in various patches near the winding source of the Bruar. At the right of the entrance to the pass, the lonely dwelling called Bruar Lodge lies a mere speck beneath Ben Dearg ... Down winds the Bruar through the glen, sometimes creeping silently through the mossy stones, at others raving maddening and bearing all before it. Nearby, in front of the Lodge is a wooden foot bridge raised high above the water so as to give it a free passage. Some distance up the glen, towards the east, a lofty cataract falls from the mountain side and the head of the glen is obstructed by a chain of mountains'.

It was the Minigaig road that brought prosperity to Glen Bruar and along its length there were numerous settlements and further up, an extensive shieling network. The opening of the military road in 1729 deprived the glen of one of its main sources of income, gave impetus to its depopulation so that today, apart from the keeper and his family living at the lodge, the glen is deserted.

Once over the ridge, the road passes through a shieling called *Allt nan Dearcag* (the bilberry stream) 835 748. The bilberry was used for dyeing a violet or purple colour and had an astringent quality useful for curing dysentry. Sometimes it would be made into tarts and jellies to which the highlanders would add whisky. In 1669 the shieling was leased to tenants of two settlements in Glen Tilt and the remains of several bothies can be seen in an expanse of green pasture on a slope above Bruar Water. In less than a mile, the road reaches Bruar Lodge, one of the Dukes' hunting seats. This was formerly situated two miles further up the glen and was rebuilt in its present place in 1789. It was named *Cabair Feidh* (deer's antler) 832 761 and according to Scrope in 1838 'consists of two small tenements facing each other encompassed by a wall so as to form a small court between them. One of these buildings serves the master and the other for his servants. There is besides a lodging place for the hill men, rather frail in structure, a dog kennel of the same picturesque character. Close by stands a black stack of peats'. Considerable alterations were carried out in 1865 and 1888. Here two shielings straddle the Bruar; *Ruidh Dorcha Mhor* (great dark shieling) 830 762 on the west side and to the east, near the Lodge, *Ruidh Dorcha Beag* (little dark shieling) which has completely disappeared. In 1861 Ruidh Dorcha Mhor was occupied by a gamekeeper, Alex Campbell, his wife and five children and the settlement was inhabited till 1880. Two hundred years earlier, in 1669, it was a shieling where the rent was 4 wedders, value £8 Scots and in 1800 it was leased to the Rev. J. Stewart, Minister of Blair, for £40 Sterling. The footings of five dwellings can still be seen in the ground in a broad sweep of the Bruar and these were pulled down and used as material to build two sheep fanks.

Within half a mile the road passes Loch Bruar, a man-made loch formed for trout-fishing in 1912 and after a further mile, passes another shieling on the east side, in a patch of green pasture below *Creag na h-Iolair Bheag* (little rock of the eagle). This shieling was called *Ruidh na Gaoithe* (windy shieling) 823 783 and is the site of the old Bruar Lodge, where a substantial ruin measures 70 feet by 14 feet in width. Across the river are the footings of six rectangular buildings each side of *Allt Cam a' Choire Mor* (crooked burn of the great corrie) 817 790, surrounded by a stone dyke. This was a new shieling formed at the end of the 18th century and leased to the Rev. James McLagan, Minister of Blair. In 1807 the two Bruar keepers,

Wild and desolate Glen Bruar seen from the air, with the track to Bruar Lodge on the left of the river. The Minigaig passes this way, reaches Bruar Lodge below the two plantations of trees and proceeds to the head of the glen before crossing the flat upland Grampian plateau at a height of over 2,700 feet.

Charles Fraser and Robert Cameron, heard a shot and saw two men at this shieling drag a deer up the hillside and conceal it under the heather. They promptly went to the bothy in the shieling where they found Alex McDonald, shepherd from Gaick whom they charged with killing the deer. This he denied and went home. After spending the night in the bothy, the two keepers set off to find the deer but when they arrived at the spot, it had gone. They pursued the matter all the way to Gaick and there Alex McDonald admitted he had shot the deer, and moved it at dead of night to the house of a person whose name he would not divulge. The bothy the keepers spent the night in became known as 'Watcher's Bothy' and was occupied till the turn of the century to prevent deer poaching.

Head of Glen Bruar

In less than half a mile the road reaches the head of the glen, and the major obstruction on the route, a ridge called *Uchd na h-Analach* (breathless slope) 819 805, which blocks the way

Bruar Lodge beside the river and eight miles along the track from Calvine, was built in 1789 and later considerably enlarged. William Scrope was a famous tenant of the shooting lodge for ten year from 1824. He was recommended to the 4th Duke by Sir Walter Scott who described him as being 'not only a perfect gentleman, and incapable of indulging his love of sport otherwise than as he becomes one, but that he is a man of highly cultivated taste and understanding as well as much accomplishments'.

through. The Minigaig is clearly visible swinging round to the right and mounting the steep slope where a climb of 500 feet is quickly achieved. As it climbs, it has been carved out of the hillside, a major feat for those early road builders. Parts have been washed away by mountain torrents but in places it is in good order, especially near watercourses of which there are three, indicating that at this point the road was 10 feet wide. Once up the slope, the unique feature of the Minigaig becomes apparent, because this is the start of a three-mile plateau, at a height of over 2,500 feet, to the Pass and here the route is clear and marked with quartz-capped cairns along its length. Just off the road there is a fine 6-foot cairn on top of *Uchd a' Chlarsair* (harper's upland) which is appropriately named *Fidler's Cairn* 815 819. The *Caochan Lub* (meandering stream) flows below the Cairn and appears in a 16th century manuscript thus: 'The Stryp that crouketh so oft upon the heid of the wild mounth and hills of Mynygegg is called Keuchan-vin-Lowib. It runneth to Atholl . . .' It also appears in Moll's map of 1725 as Kichan Clouban and in Roy's Survey 25 years later as Kichan na Lub.

A solitary bothy 810 820 stood at the confluence of two rivers and this was part of the Caochan Lub shieling leased to Aeneas MacPherson of Killihuntly from Glen Tromie towards the end of the 17th century. A letter from Aeneas to the Marquis of Atholl dated 24 June 1696, reads as follows:

> 'My Lord, Being straitened for want of hill grass, I by this letter make my address and seek the liberties of Graisseing from your land any place lest prejudical to your Lordship's interest and most convenient for me. I am content to pay yearly and I shall not stay above a fortnight, nor go to it before July'.

His request was granted and by 1704 he was confirming the warrant by John, 1st Duke of Atholl, 'to pasture and grass my goods in His Grace's shiell called Krichanaloup lying to the north side of Glen Bruar'. But in the same year, the factor was checking up on his shieling tenants, as shown by this memorandum of 22 September:

> 'Killiehuntly shealls in the shealings of Coachannaluib and Madhuy, which are about a mile distant which two places being very prejudicial to the deer, they being the very nursery of them and which the harts ordinarily frequent till the time of their copuling with the hinds. It is said he keeps a great many cattle there not only in his own name but under the name of Bowmen, who sheall thereon likewise and that this year he will have about 57 head of cattle. It is informed that he kills a great many deer in the forests having hired of late the best deer-stalker in the two counties'.

The immediate result of this was that Aeneas was restricted to pasturing no more than 30-40 head of cattle on the shieling and he promised his men would stop taking guns and dogs into the deer forest and he would employ only a bowman and dairymaid at the shieling under a penalty of 500 merks. Two years later, the Duke was granting another warrant to Aeneas:

> 'to pasture or grass his goods in our shiell called Kuchan na Loup, and likewise we appoint him to be our fforrester for North the water of Tarff, he always performing to us the duty and services belonging to a fforrester. And for his encouragement we allow him to kill for his own use two deer yearly'.

The head of Glen Bruar is marked by a ridge called Uchd na h-Analach where the Minigaig climbs steeply to the right, quickly gaining another 500 feet to achieve a height of 2,500 feet. Watercourses at regular intervals up the slope have ensured that this part of the track remained in good condition until recently.

This arrangement continued until 1723.

Minigaig Summit

Continuing across the plateau, the road dips down to cross *Allt Glac nan Uan* (stream of the hollow of the lamb) 817 827 by means of a ford, the name reflecting the extensive grazing of sheep here in the summer months. The track is clearly marked for the final mile of the plateau and climbs gently to the summit through open land with few features. The summit is reached at a height of 2,745 feet at the *Coire Bhran* (raven's corrie) 812 847, a meeting place for drovers who, having travelled from many parts of northern Scotland, would wait here before passing through Atholl as a formidable body of men and livestock. The view from the summit is spectacular, across to Speyside and beyond, but in winter the Minigaig had a particularly bad reputation and claimed many victims. The Blair Atholl Kirk Session minutes for 13 October 1771

The old sign to the Minigaig Pass at Calvine on the old A9 pointing the way to Bruar Lodge, where it meets the Minigaig Pass route.

reported that: 'The Session appointed 16sh. Sterling for coffins and dead cloaths for the two women that were lost upon a rapid-burn this side of Minigaig going back to the North from Lothian shearing.' The danger of the supernatural was also present. *Sithean* (fairy knolls) are numerous and Raven's Corrie and Black Dog are names of evil omen. *Sithean a Choin Dubh* (fairy hills of the black dog) combines two of these and relate to a 16th century Perthshire practice when a fierce dog was specially bred to hunt down the outlawed MacGregors.

The descent on the north side begins at once, down the grassy slope, following Allt Coire Bhran as it takes a great sweep to the west and within a few miles there is a large settlement called *Ruigh nam Plaidean* (shieling of the plaids) 781 895, where the remains of eleven buildings and a sheepfold can be seen. The plaids woven here were probably not tartan, but blankets and coarse flannel. Lower down there was a small wooden factory for making bobbins from birch or alder which flourished in the glen and which would have been sold to this shieling. The road follows Allt Bhran for another mile and joins the track from Gaick Lodge at *Bhran Bridge* 763 903.

On the tongue of land at the confluence of the Bhran and Tromie there was a settlement where the remains of five buildings and an enclosure can be seen. In Blaeu's Atlas published in 1654 the name Cromlaid appears at this spot but is more likely to apply to a rocky outcrop further down the glen called Croidh-la. Across its face is a large and unusual rock formation, best seen from Kingussie five miles distant. It extends across the hill for about half a mile and is in the shape of a horse facing south. It is light grey in colour, offset by the darker background of the hill face. In a short while the Minigaig passes *Bhran Cottage* 753 914, roofed and still used by the estate, lying in a sweep of the Tromie which it fords to join up with Comyn's Road for the final five miles to Ruthven.

There is one reminder of this once great Grampian thoroughfare – a sign at Calvine, five miles north of Blair Atholl – which says 'Minigaig Pass to Speyside', pointing the way to the track to Bruar Lodge and beyond.

CHAPTER 3

The Military Road

Had you seen these roads before they were made
You would lift up your hands and bless General Wade.

Military roads in the Highlands were built with a view to the preservation of law and order in the districts they served. Roads have always been the pioneer in the development and establishment of authority in all countries and so we find the first roads worthy of the name in the Highlands were military, which opened up the land and enabled the law to be enforced. Before Wade, there were no roads as such in the Highlands and according to Burt, 'the old ways (for roads I shall not call them) consisted chiefly of stony moors, bogs, rugged rapid fords, declivities of the hills, entangling woods and giddy precipices.'

After the two insurrections of 1715 and 1719 the Highlands were in turmoil. The active part taken by many of the clan chiefs in supporting either the Hanoverian or Pretender's cause encouraged fighting between these rivals. The Disarming Act of 1717 was not working because the loyal clans, having surrendered their arms, were at the mercy of their more aggressive neighbours who had refused to do so. In 1724 conditions became intolerable for the government which decided to take measures to stamp out the lawlessness then rampant all over the Highlands. Accordingly, George I instructed Wade to proceed north to report on the situation. Wade received his instructions on 3rd July 1724:

'Narrowly to inspect the situation of the Highlanders, their manners, customs, the state of the Country in regard to the Dominions, to make special enquiry into the allegations that the effect of the Disarming Act had been to leave the loyal party in the Highlands naked and defenceless at the mercy of the disloyal . . . and suggest to the King such stern remedies as may conduce to the quiet of His Majesty's faithful subjects, and the good settlement of that part of the Kingdom.'

George Wade was born in Ireland in 1673 and gazetted an ensign in the 10th Foot, Earl of Bath's Regiment in 1690. Promotion was rapid as he was made a lieutenant in 1694 and captain a year later. He distinguished himself at the siege of Liège in Flanders in 1702 where with his grenadiers he stormed and carried the citadel and was promoted to Lieutenant-General. In 1708 he was sent to Spain as second-in-command of an expedition to Minorca and encountered great difficulty in transporting the army siege guns as the ground was both rough and mountainous. Here he probably had his first experience of road-making as Minorca, like the Highlands had no roads. He was promoted Major-General in 1711 and given the command of Ireland and in 1722 was elected Member of Parliament for Bath.

Wade set off for Scotland next day and submitted a lengthy report on 10th December in which he stated that:

'The Highlands in Scotland are still more impracticable from the want of roads, bridges and from the excessive rains that almost continually fall in these parts, which by nature and constant use become habitual to the natives, but very difficultly supported by the regular troops. They are unacquainted with the passages by which the mountains are traversed, exposed to frequent ambuscades and shot from the tops of the hills.'

He made no recommendation until April of the following year that roads should be constructed, when he wrote a supplement to his report in which he mentioned the need for 'mending the roads between the garrisons and barracks for the better communication of His Majesty's troops'. Within two weeks Wade was appointed Commander of the Forces in North Britain and returned to Scotland in June 1725. Road construction started the following year and continued for 11 years by which time 240 miles had been completed.

Wade followed the Roman principle of keeping to a straight line except when climbing steep gradients, where he built a series of sharp bends. The standard width was 16 feet though this varied from 30 feet in the south to 10 feet in the north. Five hundred soldiers were employed from May to October; privates being paid an additional 6d a day for their labours, corporals 8d, sergeants 1/-, while officers received an extra 2/6d. Barrack huts were erected at regular intervals to house the soldiers and these in turn developed into inns or change-houses, became known as King's Houses and were finally established every 10 miles. Stone pillars 'to prevent the travellers being deceived in rain, snow, drift or approaching night', were set up every five miles. The Wade Stone, north of Dalnacardoch is the only remaining marker stone in the parish. When traversing bogs, the loose ground was excavated down to the gravel floor and the hollow filled with a layer of large stones, then smaller sizes to fill the gaps and finally gravel to form a smooth surface. When passing along slopes, the road was usually dug into the hillside with a drain on the inside. At first no bridges were built, suitable places being selected for fords which were cleared across the rivers by removing the large stones, but subsequent spates brought down more boulders. Bridges did not keep pace with road construction, possibly because of a scarcity of artificers and the early ones were of timber which were slowly replaced by stone. An account of tools for building roads included 200 iron spades, 200 iron shovels and 200 wooden shovels of similar size, 300 pickaxes each 26 inches long including the eye which had to be very strong, 120 pickaxe handles as well as sledge-hammers, Jackson handscrews, barrows and iron and steel weights. As the work was being carried out on rough, stony terrain, there was a request for better quality tools than those supplied the previous year.

In September 1727 Wade started planning his great road, from Inverness to Perth 'which will open up a Communication with the low country and facilitate the march of a body of troops when His Majesty's service may require it' and the following month he submitted an eight-part proposal for his future plans for road building.

> Part I covers the road through Atholl: 'A military way may be made through the mountains from Inverness southwards as far as Perth which will open up a short and speedy communication with the troops quartered in the low country; contribute to civilise the Highlands and in my humble opinion, prove the most effective means to continue them in a due obedience to Your Majesty's Government'. Part VI covers the expenses of building this road in the first year: 'That the same allowance of £1,000 out of the contingencys of the army be continued for the ensuing year for making of a road or military way from Inverness by Ruthven in Badenoch as far as Perth, for the march of troops, wheel carriage or cannon'. Part VII proposed 'that a stable for 30 horses be erected at the Barrack of Ruthven, which being near the middle of the Highlands and the road proposed in the preceding article, I conceive to be a proper station for a party of dragoons to serve as a convoy for money or provisions for the use of the forces as well as to retain that part of ye country in obedience'. Part VIII of the proposal requested £600 a year for two years for building stone bridges 'over rivers and other torrents of water that fall from the mountains, by which passengers frequently lose their lives and the troops are often intercepted in their marches for several days successively'.

In 1728 Wade started construction of the military road from Inverness to Perth and in his letter to the Secretary of State of 20th July, told him of his progress:

This extract from James Dorret's map entitled 'A general Map of
Scotland and Islands' dated 1750 clearly shows the Military road
passing through Blair and proceeding in a north-westerly direction
beside the River Garry to Drumochter. Wade's road to the south-west
branches off at Dalnacardoch, passes through Trinafour, climbs over
the hill to Tummel Bridge and proceeds by Aberfeldy to Crieff.

'I am now with all possible diligence carrying on the new road for
wheel carriages between Dunkeld and Inverness of about 80
English miles in length and that no time may be lost in a work so
necessary for His Majesty's Service, I have employed 300 men on
different parts of the road, that the work may be done during this
favourable season of the year, and hope by the progress they have
already made, to have 40 miles of it compleated before the end of
October, at which time the heavy rains make it impracticable to
proceed with the work till the summer following. There is so great
a scarcity of provisions in this barren country that I am obliged to
bring my biscuits, cheese etc . . . for the support of the workmen,
from Edinburgh by land carriage which though expensive is of
absolute necessity. There is about 15 miles of this road compleatly
finished and I may venture to assure you it is as good as practicable
for wheel carriages as any in England'.

In April 1729 the Treasury advanced £2,915 to finish the road
and £670 of that was for building 11 stone bridges of one arch,
each 15 to 26 feet wide and in October of the same year the
road was finished, an event celebrated with a feast at Oxbridge,

near Dalnaspidal. In the following year Wade started building
the route to the south-west from Dalnacardoch through
Tummel Bridge to Crieff.

Conditions

Reports of the condition of the roads in the 1730s were
favourable. Burt in his letters records that 'the roads on these
moors are now as smooth as Constitution Hill and I have
galloped on some of them for miles in great tranquility', while a
Scottish gentleman visiting the Highlands in 1737 was
surprised by the improvements he found and gratefully noted
the existence of inns along the route for the entertainment of
travellers. But these early Wade roads were not very durable
and as early as 1738 Edward Caulfeild, who was allowed £400 a
year for maintenance, had to repair the road from Crieff to
Inverness. '100 miles in length and new gravell'd the same is
wanting' is his description of what seems to be a major
reconstruction. Wade relinquished his Scottish command in
1740 and was succeeded by Lieutenant General Jasper Clayton
and later military road-making came under Sir John Cope in
1744. Edward Caulfeild remained superintendent and
surveyor until 1769 and many military roads were made under
his supervision until 1750, after which few were built.

These roads were dependent on the War Office for their
maintenance and repair and from 1770 to 1783 the budget for
this service was £7,000 per annum. This dwindled to £4,700 for
the next 20 years and then £5,500 for the following ten. To
Wade's contemporaries his roads must have seemed a
masterpiece of engineering skill but the next generation was
less satisfied with them, as it was beginning to dawn on the
statesmen of the time that they could have a political and
economic value as well. Much of the money was spent on
making improvements or diverting the roads by making new
cuts. In some cases a new line was made because the original
was liable to be destroyed by landslide or rendered impassable
by flooding. There were dangerous passes where the road was
barely 10 feet wide without parapets and gradients of 1 in 4,
especially at the County March and Dalnacardoch. These
repairs were carried out by an inspector, 16 overseers, master
masons and 270 labourers who worked during the summer.

In 1770 Colonel Robert Skene was placed in charge of road building and maintenance and immediately made plans for improving the road. A new and easier line was planned between Bruar and Dalnacardoch and a stretch south of Dalnaspidal moved further up the hillside to overcome severe flooding problems. By 1775 all the bridges had been repaired and in that year the Colonel 'behaved very genteely' when approached by the Atholl estate for more men to be posted to the Dalnacardoch stretch. 'If Colonel Skene would build the bridges this year upon the new road to Dallnacardich I believe we might have it opened this winter but without the bridges it would be impassable', commented the factor.

Parliamentary Roads

In 1798 it was decreed that the roads were no longer necessary for military purposes and money provided by Parliament for maintaining them was withdrawn. The Highland Society met in Edinburgh on 8th January 1799 and immediately formed a committee which reported back on the situation in April. The committee maintained there were two ways of providing funds; 'levying tolls and statute labour'. The first method they said would scarcely cover the costs of collection as travellers were so few and because of the importance of these roads, statute labour should be provided, funded from county sources.

> 'If they are not kept in repair without public aid, the communication betwixt the Highlands of Scotland and Southern parts will, in a great degree, be at an end, to the equal disadvantage of both, as the South receives annually, by the conveyance of these roads, a great supply of sheep, cattle, wool and other articles from the Northern and Highland districts'.

At this time the Government was becoming increasingly alarmed at the rising emigration level in the Highlands. Landlords were finding that by putting their lands under sheep it was three times as profitable as when it was under black cattle. Sheep required less labour and landless crofters were emigrating with their families to America. Thomas Telford was therefore instructed to visit and investigate the area and submitted his report in 1802. One of his remedial measures

A stretch of the Great North Road north of Dalnacardoch in 1924, with the main railway line to Inverness and the River Garry on the left. At this time it was still a rough track which had changed little since the 1820s.

was 'to make the intercourse of the Country more perfect by the construction of good roads and bridges'. A year later, a Board of Parliamentary Commissioners received Royal assent under an Act 'for granting the sum of £20,000 to be used and applied towards making roads and building bridges in the Highlands of Scotland for enabling the proprietors of land to charge their estates with a proportion of the expenses of making and keeping in repair, roads and bridges'. Telford specified a great many drains and conduits across the roads to provide efficient drainage. The roads themselves were to be 20 feet in width except in rocky cuttings where 18 feet was permitted and the surface was to be gravel, with no stone larger than a 'hen's egg', to be laid to a depth of 14 inches in the middle and 9 inches at the sides. These roads were to be built to suit the commercial and agricultural interests of the land owners, who would derive considerable benefit from them and in consequence, they were to bear half the cost, with the counties providing the balance.

The County of Perthshire refused to incur these costs and the roads were left for a number of years with no maintenance as they argued there were stretches of 15 – 20 miles with few houses and these districts would be quite incapable of funding any repairs. In 1819 the Commission considered the necessity of repairing the road between Dunkeld and the County March, a distance of 40 miles. They reported that:

'The state of the road requires renewal rather than repair. Its importance is so great that almost any degree of difficulty ought to be encountered in order to put it into as good a state of repair as that of any of the roads to and from which it communicates with Edinburgh. It will cost more than twice as much to repair this long neglected road for all the Highland roads will become insulated as soon as this portion of the road becomes impassable, which will probably happen before the end of the present year. Indeed it may be said to have happened already, a bridge having very recently fallen and two others being in so dangerous a state that the coach, with its horses, does not venture a passage and the coach is pulled over these bridges by men'.

By 1820 the road was virtually impassable and the Duke of Atholl applied to the Commission for John Mitchell to arrange its repair. He immediately surveyed the road and submitted a lengthy report on its condition and an estimate of costs to repair it. The report makes interesting reading as it gives an idea of the state of the military road at this time and remedial measures necessary to repair it. That part of the report relating to the section in Atholl now follows:

'Report and estimate, for repairing the road from the boundary of Inverness-shire, to Dunkeld with a view of making it passable in safety, at the least possible expense'.

Section 1		April 1820	
This section extends from the end of Badenoch Road to Dalnacardoch and measures 8 miles. The repairs are to consist in removing the large stones from the surface, filling the hollows and wheel tracks, clearing the water cources and covering the whole road with gravel to the depth of 4 inches, at £30 per mile.	£ 240	s 0	d 0
80 cross drains to be made with necessary embankments and back drains at 50/- each	200	0	0
Repairing the bridges in this section	100	0	0
	£540	0	0

Section II
From the end of the last section
proceeding Southwards 3 miles, the
surface is covered with large stones,
rocky points and irregular hollows,
which must be removed and being
too low in the middle, it requires

	£	s	d			
4 inches of good gravel and will cost £36 per mile	108	0	0			
20 cross drains, with embanking and back drains at 40/- each	40	0	0			
				£148	0	0

Section III
From end of last lot for another
mile Southward, the road is very
irregular, and hollow in the middle,
and requires 10 inches of gravel all
the way, which must be carted and

	£	s	d			
the water cources made at 1/3 per yard	110	0	0			
4 covered drains to be made, with embanking	6	0	0			
The building and repairing bridges in this, and the foregoing section	210	0	0			
				£326	0	0

Section IV
From end of last lot to the arable
land of Dalriavish, being ½ mile, the
road passes over a variety of rocky
ridges, from 6 to 18 inches above
the general surface. These must be
partly removed and gravel laid to

	£	s	d			
that depth, which must be carted at 1/6 per yard.	198	0	0			
5 covered drains, with back drains, at 30/-	7	10	0			
				£205	10	0

Section V
From the end of last section, to the
bridge beyond Bruar, being about
½ mile, the road surface is in pretty
good form but there are many large
stones to be removed and the
surface covered with good gravel,

	£	s	d			
to the depth of 4 inches water cources cleared will cost 4d per yard	44	0	0			
Bridges and cross drains to be repaired	30	0	0			
				£74	0	0

Section VI
From thence to the milestone
North of Blair Inn being 2½ miles,
the road most of the way is cut
irregular and hollow in the middle,
and in some places covered with
large stones, these must be removed
and gravel carted, and laid over it,
to the average depth of 6 inches at
6d yard   £110   0   0

Section VII
From the said milestone, proceeding
Southward for 4 miles, the road in
some places is steep, and the whole
gravel washed off, which other
parts is covered with mud, large
stones and very irregular.

	£	s	d			
It will require 10 inches of gravel, all the way, which must be carted and will cost 1/4d yard	469	6	8			
Bridges and drains to be repaired	80	0	0			
				£549	6	8

	£	s	d
Estimate for Atholl section	£1,952	16	8

Mitchell's plan assumed that the route taken by the military road
to the north of the castle would be followed, but this meant
crossing by the old Bridge of Tilt, then in a ruinous state and also
the road between it and Blair was dangerously steep. Therefore
the possibility of changing the route was raised at this time to

The same stretch of road north of Dalnacardoch seen in 1930 after it had been surfaced for the first time.

reduce the distance by 1½ miles in three. One proposal was to renew the military road through the castle grounds as far as the East Lodge, and then utilise the road through the policies, to the 'new inn' of Blair and turn east to a new Tilt Bridge. This idea was rejected by the Duke and a new line was drawn up taking the road between the Garry and the Castle which is the road we use through Blair Atholl today.

By 1821 Mitchell reported that the road from the County March to Bruar had been satisfactorily repaired 'and the whole surface, water courses, and buildings are at present in a very excellent state excepting the corners of three bridges which had been injured by carts striking against the parapets.' As the season was too far advanced, the bridges would have to be temporarily repaired till spring, 'when they will be pointed or rough cast and guard stones placed to prevent carts coming into contact with them'. Mitchell was satisfied with the road surface on the stretch from Bruar to the Deer Park in the castle grounds, which he said needed little attention. But there was still concern about the two heights at the County March and Dalnacardoch and at a meeting of the Trustees of the Atholl Turnpike Road Committee, chaired by the Duke of Atholl, Mitchell was asked to reduce them because of a growing interest in attracting the mail service to use this line to reach Inverness, rather than the present way through Aberdeen. So on 13th May 1825 Mitchell was able to report the road in good condition and the surface 'properly dressed up'. Later that year however, he was reporting that several watercourses under the bridges had become choked with rubbish and had to be cleared without delay. The improvements continued and in 1827 a new line of about ½ mile was planned near the Edendon Toll, where 50 men were employed to finish the job before the winter set in. The road at this point was described as being 'inconveniently steep and affected with snow in winter'. The new road from Dalnaspidal to the County March was described as 'one of the greatest improvements imaginable, its fine level and breadth all along is beyond description, doing away with the three greatest hills on all the road.'

Tolls

In June 1820 a decision was taken to levy tolls on the road from the County March to Bruar and directions issued to build two, one at the March itself and the other at Dalnacardoch. The *March Toll* 632 760 was built on the right-hand side of the road going north and 50 yards south of the boundary on level ground with a small stream nearby where it was protected by a low ridge. A bog lay below the site and a strong dyke, 100 yards long, was built between the ridge and the gable-end of the house, to prevent evasion. John Walker, Glen Bruar forester, offered to build a cottage here at a cost of £100, from money borrowed from the estate at 7½% interest and agreed to lodge and assist the Duke's gamekeepers and foxhunters when in the area and keep the marches clear of Badenoch cattle. He would undertake this in return for 'keeping a dram for passengers and for lodging stormbound travellers'. It was not until 1830 that a licence to sell spirits and ale was granted for the County March toll house. John Stewart, a relative of Convener Dr. Stewart was appointed to the *Edendon Toll* 715 707 north of Dalnacardoch and in June 1821, toll bars and gates were in place with painted regulation boards in hand and both tolls became operational in July of that year. Tolls were let to the highest bidder, the County March lease being £137 per annum while Edendon was set at £77. During the first year the County March took in £162.4.11¼ in tolls and Edendon

£99.9.7½. Toll rates were levied on everything that passed, save pedestrians:

	1821	1827
Carriages drawn by two horses	1/6	2/-
Gigs	7d	9d
Saddle horses	2½d	3d
Carriers for hire with carts	8d	1/-

September and October were the most popular months, drawing a third of total takings. This was the height of the droving season and drovers were charged 10d per score of cattle and 4d per score of sheep, though the rates at Edendon were half this. A year later, a decision was taken to build a third toll house at *Bruar* 822 659 which was leased to Donald Forbes for £75 per annum and started in December 1822 when £3.11.3 was taken during that month. By then, the Caledonian Coach Company was running a regular service between Inverness and Perth though tolls were not collected at the toll bars but direct from the coach proprietors.

Examination of the Atholl Turnpike Road Fund showed the importance of attracting the mail coach as a means of providing extra revenue.

Prospectus of Atholl Turnpike Funds Whit 1837

Funds

		£	s	d
1.	Sum in Bank at Whit. 1836	1,005	0	1½
2.	Let of Bars for year to Whit. 1837	1,074	0	0
3.	Caledonian Coach to 15th May 1837	25	16	0
4.	Mail coach to 15th May 1837	293	19	0
5.	Interest on Bank account, say	20	0	0
		£2,418	15	1½

Payments

		£	s	d
1. Maintaining Road		535	12	6
2. Alterations and improvements		478	2	0
3. Fences and repairs and sundries at toll houses		69	9	0
4. Interest on loans		450	0	0
5. General and local superintendents		79	4	0
6. Clerk and treasurer		40	0	0
7. Miscellanies say		40	0	0
		£1,692	7	6
Surplus		£726	7	7½

Toll bars were abolished in 1879 and the seven tolls in various parts of the Atholl estate were bought for £500 as the coming of the railway caused much of the traffic to be diverted and the tolls became uneconomic.

Coach Services

Before 1800 there was no coach service in the Highlands and in that year an attempt to establish one between Inverness and Perth had to be abandoned because of the state of the road. At a meeting of Vintners in 1804 it was decided to 'establish a diligence or stagecoach to go regularly three times a week between Inverness and Perth' and they were informed that a grant from the Military Road Fund might be available for 'keeping the road in the hill of Drumochter free of snow or at least in a passable state during the winter months'. By 1806 the first regular coach service had been established and the Caledonian Coach Company was running a twice-weekly service to Edinburgh, reduced to once a week in winter and taking three days for the journey. In 1811 they announced a summer service running five days a week which reduced the journey to two days, when passengers were allowed a seven-hour stop for the night they were on the road. In 1820 they improved their winter service, coaches to Perth running three times a week and the journey taking a day. Innkeepers along the route were contracted to change horses at every stage and passengers were given ample time for breakfast and lunch. The coach left Inverness on Mondays, Wednesdays and Fridays and from Perth on Tuesdays, Thursdays and Saturdays, starting at 5 a.m. and arriving at 10 p.m. In 1826 a daily coach service was running between the George and Star Hotel, Perth and the Caledonian Hotel, Inverness. By 1836 the Post Office was looking favourably at the route through the Grampians for transport of mail. The old route to Inverness was along the coast through Aberdeen and was a journey of 200 miles, nearly double the military road route and consequently taking an

Duke of Wellington Coach Timetable 1844

			Distance
Depart:	Inverness	10.00 pm	
Arrive:	Frieburn	11.50 pm	16
	Carrbridge	12.50 am	9
	Aviemore	1.37 am	7
	Kingussie	3.07 am	12
	Dalwhinnie	4.45 am	14
	Dalnacardoch	6.19 am	13
	Blair Atholl	7.33 am	11
	Breakfast (20 mins)		
	Pitlochrie	8.39 am	7
	Moulinearn	8.59 am	3
	Dunkeld	10.03 am	10
	Auchtergaven	10.48 am	6.4 furlongs
	Perth	11.40 am	8.4 furlongs
		13.40 hours	117 miles

Depart:	Perth	6.00 am	
Arrive:	Auchtergaven	6.50 am	
	Dunkeld	7.35 am	
	Moulinearn	8.39 am	
	Breakfast (20 mins)		
	Pitlochrie	9.19 am	
	Blair Atholl	10.05 am	
	Dalnacardoch	11.19 am	
	Dalwhinnie	12.33 pm	
	Kingussie	2.31 pm	
	Aviemore	4.01 pm	
	Carrbridge	4.46 pm	
	Frieburn	6.16 pm	
	Inverness	8.00 pm	
		14 hours	

extra 20 hours. With all the improvements undertaken, the first mail coach from Perth to Inverness ran in 1836 and by then the journey had been reduced to little more than 12 hours. The service was short-lived as the Post Office withdrew it when the main railway line to Inverness via Nairn and the east coast was opened in 1856.

It is interesting to note the precise 20 minute breakfast stop in Blair Atholl on the journey south and Moulinearn on the way north in the 1844 schedule for the Duke of Wellington Coach.

Problems of travel in those days are recorded in various newspaper accounts of the time. In March 1808, the 'Highland Road,' which had been completely blocked by snow all winter, was opened to travellers, yet in 1823 following a very heavy snowstorm, it was noted that the road was open while the east coast road was impassable. In 1826 three of the coaches became snowed up on the road and at the County March the top of one of them was all that was visible. In 1841 it was closed for six weeks because of severe snow storms and only with difficulty was a horse track kept open.

An Alternative Route

In 1827 Joseph Mitchell was asked to survey a new line for the road, resulting in a saving of 20 miles between Inverness and Perth. A glance at the map shows the military road route in the shape of an inverted 'S' with the two bulges formed by Drumochter and Aviemore. Mitchell, after surveying the ground, submitted two alternatives, one of which left the present road a few miles south of Aviemore, proceeded up Glen Tromie past Loch an t-Seilich and climbed up Allt Gharbh Ghaig, before descending into Glen Bruar to reach Blair Atholl a mile north of the Tilt Bridge. He supported this route by instancing a journey undertaken by two acquaintances on horseback. They left Kingussie at 6 a.m. crossed the Grampians by way of the Minigaig Pass and arrived in Blair Atholl at 10 a.m. The Duke of Atholl was surprised to hear about plans to shorten and improve the road maintaining it would be impracticable as the road would only be used for a short period throughout the year and this would make even the cost of a survey unwarrantable. His letter continued:

A 1930 view of the Edendon Toll, north of Dalnacardoch, established in 1821 and closed in 1879. Tollkeepers, fearing loss of revenue by drovers using Glen Bruar to avoid paying dues, often reported the size of the droves as they approached Atholl.

'The track from Blair Atholl to Minigaig was only a drove track. The first part from Blair Atholl to Glen Bruar is rather better and could have been a rough wheel track but the latter part over the top of the hill to the County March is difficult to follow and merely a track marked with stones. The gradient alone necessary to get up to the top would knock it out for any purpose of haulage'.

Mitchell maintained that the method of construction of the military road – excavating to gravel level with high banks – was satisfactory in summer but in winter it formed a 'complete receptacle of snow'. He argued that 'the road across the Minigaig would be raised up on an embankment and as it was in an open, exposed situation there would be no blockage of snow as the wind, which normally causes drifting, would keep the road clear'.

The Inverness Town Clerk, who signed himself 'VIATOR' wrote a number of letters mentioning the benefits of the new route. He said that the frequent repairs and changes to the military road reminded him of the story of the coat which had been patched and mended so often that little of the original remained. He argued the present road was 'fundamentally bad, being very narrow with many acute angles and precipitous descents, many without parapets. The radical objection however is to the line of roads as circuitous – It is quite serpentine-like'. The new route would have saved at least two days in the transportation of sheep and cattle.

There was much resistance to this scheme, especially from landlords along the military road who maintained the projected road would be impassable for five months every year and even in summer 'dangerous from the frequent storms and perpetual fogs which give its name to the mountains'. Then it transpired that Robertson, the Town Clerk, had a 26-acre estate which would benefit considerably from the new road. On 21st November 1828 he advertised the Dalmigavie shooting ground to let on his farm and as a further inducement to would-be tenants, stated in his advertisement that 'the new road is to pass through the hill ground'. Even in 1829 he was still advertising his estate with the added inducement, 'upon the new projected line of the Highland Road', though by this time the Parliamentary Commissioners had discovered the deception and abandoned the scheme. Support for the military road came from the editor of the *Caledonian Mercury* who wrote in his columns that the new line would interfere with the private interests of landowners, as the present road passed through their lands and could not be kept up when the tolls were removed by this 'cold and visionary road. It is nothing less than a demand to sacrifice a great public good for the sake of a paltry private profit to a few individuals'. The *Scotsman* was a supporter of the new route, stating that it was absurd to doubt the success of the road as the most eminent engineer in the country has staked his reputation on it. 'It is inconsistent to object that this 'wild' road would annihilate the other'. Those opposed to the road insisted that with the removal of the tolls, the present road would become impassable very quickly and no amount of repair or tolls would prevent the new line from becoming blocked in winter and with both roads closed, there would be no communication with the south. In the end, lack of funds and objections about the great height of the new line and the desolate countryside on its route, put this plan out of the question.

In only 60 years the Great North Road has changed from a rough track to a two lane highway and now in the 1980s a dual carriageway. Here it is seen at the Wade Stone south of Dalnaspidal.

The 20th Century

As the 19th century drew to a close, the parliamentary road was used less and less as the railway opened in 1863 and increased in popularity, until the coming of the motor car. This brought traffic demands and financial consequences which the authorities were unable to meet and once again the Government decided to improve the road which had changed little over the previous 100 years. In May 1925, a major reconstruction and surfacing project started, again under a military man, Major Robert Bruce, who was appointed resident engineer with the remit to control, construct and complete the road. The work was seriously delayed by the General Strike of 1926 and excessively wet winters (the worst for 40 years) which were experienced during 1927 and 1928, the year of completion of what until recently was the old A9. ·

Rapid growth of car ownership and its use for leisure purposes together with haulage vehicles increasing in both size and number, brought more and more demands on the roads, and the one to Inverness was no exception due particularly to the growth in Scottish tourism. It was evident by the mid 1960s that extensive improvements would again be required. The route and gradients were still totally inadequate to cope with the volume of traffic in summer; the journey time from Perth to Inverness was unacceptably long, and problems caused by severe weather were aggravated by gradients and alignments which were below the standards demanded for current traffic requirements. Thus the pattern of centenary review of improvement was broken ahead of schedule when it was decided that an extensive 'renewal' programme was required. The difficulties encountered in the project were no different to those which faced Wade, Telford and Bruce, with a rugged and remote terrain and unfriendly, unreliable weather. As with the road builders of the 18th and 19th centuries, the scale of the task lay not only in the length of the road but in the topography, formidable climate, major river crossings and difficulty of accessibility to remote areas with construction plant. It was not until 1986 that the entire project was completed and a new trunk road established between Perth and Inverness and that included the stretch through the Pass of Killiecrankie which presented the greatest challenge to engineers in terms of design and construction.

CHAPTER FOUR

Kilmaveonaig to Baluain

The Military Road

A few hundred yards south of Ballentoul in Bridge of Tilt the Wade road goes off to the right, leaving the modern road which sweeps round the Craggan Corner, before the Blair Atholl garage on the left. At one time there were two Lude settlements here, *Western Craggan* and *Easter Craggan* (place of little rocks) 887 648. Lude was formed into a Barony by Royal Charter under the Great Seal in 1448 and occupies the land east of the River Tilt – between the Garry and the Fender. The Marquis of Atholl acquired the superiority of the Barony in 1673 from Anthony White a Writer to the Signet, for a trifling debt and Lude started paying a feu duty of 100 merks and 14 wedders, converted at £2 Scots each, two for each one of the Seven Shielings in Glen Loch. There were five Lude tenants in the Craggans and an extract from the 1759 rent book shows how this rent was paid:

Wester Craggan – A Merkland 1759

		Sterling	
	£	s	d
Donald Stewart possesses the one half of this			
Town for which he pays of money rent	2	12	6
He pays three firlots of farm bere or		7	6
Pays for baggage		4	0
Augmentation of stipend			8
	£3	4	8

He pays the following services:

	s	d
Harrows three bolls, three firlots oats	4	6
Two days darg of a man to cast peats	1	0
Days darg of a man and two horses to drive dung	1	6
Leads 17 loads of peats	1	5
Two days darg of a man to pull lint	1	0
Two days darg of a man to shear	1	0
He leads corn and hay when desired	5	0
Pays three hens	1	6
	16	11

The Wade road carries straight on but all traces have been lost in the fields below *Lude House*, Gaelic Leathad, (slope) 886 656, which was described by the Hon. Sarah Murray when visiting the area in 1796: 'A mile and a half further, I came to the foot of the hill on which Lude stands. How to get at the house I could not tell as it appeared to me that none but winged animals or scrambling goats could gain the height of Lude'. Originally the principal dwelling house of the Robertson of Lude family was situated high up Glen Fender, across the river from Kirkton of Lude but around 1650 the family moved down the glen. A new drive with lodge and imposing entrance was built in 1830 to link up with the recently constructed parliamentary road following the disuse of the Wade road at this point, and Lude House at Balnagrew was completely rebuilt and enlarged at the same time.

In half a mile the road passes through Kilmaveonaig, at one time a settlement with ten houses and barns clustered around the church. This was the village where the Red Comyn developed a taste for Atholl ale in the 13th century. The school house stood to the east of the church and remained for a few years after other houses became empty. New cottages were built beside the new road at Ballentoul and gradually the old village fell into decay and all that remains now is the church which became a place of Episcopal worship. In another half mile, again across fields, the road arrives at Old Bridge of Tilt, where an inn was situated on the right, where the old sawmill now stands. With the diversion of the main road in the 1820s Lude contracted to build an inn near the new Bridge of Tilt for £1,400 and the landlord of the old inn was offered a lease of the new one, now known as the Tilt Hotel. The old inn was an attractive thatched cottage which was pulled down in the 1930s. In 1851 Old Bridge of Tilt contained eight houses and a population of 26 including a woollen weaver, two sawmillers and a grocer.

Old Tilt Bridge

From here it is a few steps to Wade's crossing of the Tilt by the *Old Tilt Bridge* 876 663 sometimes know as the Black Bridge, site of the oldest bridge in Atholl. Called Pons Tiltae by Camden, there was a crossing here in the 16th century as it

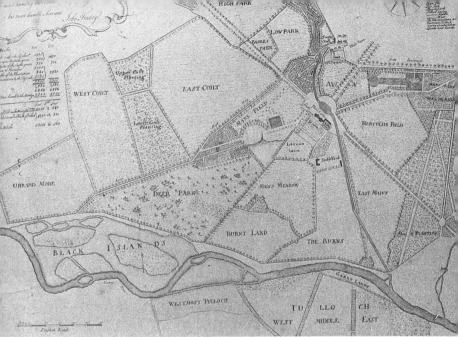

John Tinney's 1744 map of Blair Castle shows the military road passing through Blair Town (now Old Blair) and to the north of the castle. The names of some of the old settlements like Cult and Urrard, cleared when the policies were laid out in the 1730s, survive as field names on this map.

appears on the 1600 Pont manuscript map of the area. Wade constructed a stone bridge here, and when the new road was built it was removed as it was unsafe. This arose because the east end fell on Lude estate and the west side on Atholl and neither laird could agree to its repair. In 1844 Lord Glenlyon asked Mr McInroy of Lude if he could construct a temporary wooden bridge because of problems of crossing to St. Bride's Church in Old Blair. Although in ruins by that time, St. Bride's was still used for burials and to get to the funeral, villagers had to take a road which passed through the policies, coming out at Tibby's Lodge. A fine iron structure replaced the wooden bridge and in the 1980s, concrete parapets were erected on each side of the bridge.

Across the bridge, the modern road follows the Wade road beside a 7-feet high wall built in 1758 and reaches a dry arch built as a way over the road, part of a walk to a grotto 875 663 on the west bank of the Tilt, described by Robert Heron in 1793:

'I was carried by my conductor by paths, the line of which I recollect not, to a grotto, in front of which poured a cataract. Within this grotto was a mossy seat – a scene where a hermit might forget the world and indulge in undisturbed meditation on the wonders of nature. Spars, several types of quartz disposed with some ores are disposed through the rude walls: from the roof hang stalactites.'

The cataract he saw is called the York Cascade, named following a visit by the Archbishop in the 17th century and is formed by the lade for the old mills in Old Bridge of Tilt, where it plunges 50 feet into the river.

In a few yards the road reaches the East Lodge, gateway to Glen Tilt and opposite the place where *Tibby's Lodge* 873 663 was situated. This was built by James, 2nd Duke, when the military road was constructed in 1728 and the arch was formed across the Wade road in 1755. The lodge was named after Tibby Cameron, the lodge-keeper. By 1880 it was falling into disrepair and was demolished in 1884 when the East Lodge was built. Beside the lodge is the north wall of Hercules Park described in 1760 by Richard Pococke, Bishop of Ossory:

'In the whole length of the kitchen garden, the Duke has made a fine place of water with six or seven islands and peninsulas in it, two of which are for swans to breed on, having thatched houses built on them for that purpose. The garden is formed on a gentle declivity all walled round. There is a pigeon house at one angle and gardener's house at another and at the south end is a semi-circular summer house which is all glass in the front. In the walk leading to this and on each side are about 20 grotesque figures. To the east of it is a fine walk with a colossal statue of Hercules in it. This is the most beautiful kitchen garden I believe in the world.'

Dorothy Wordsworth stayed in the inn in 1803 and tells us that she:

'. . . went into the gardens where there was plenty of fruit, gooseberries hanging as thick as possible upon the trees, ready to drop off. One part of the garden was decorated with statues, dressed in gay-painted clothes and in a retired corner of the grounds, under some tall trees, appeared the figure of a favourite old gamekeeper of one of the former Dukes, in the attitude of pointing his gun at the game.'

In 1731 the Duke started to improve the gardens and parks around the castle and laid out pleasure gardens. These gradually increased as the leases for the small farms around the castle expired and by 1744, all the land west of the Tilt as far as Woodend had been converted. Farms acquired and included in the policies were Urrard More, Urrard Beg, Cult More, Cult Beg, Ardindeor, Crom Raon, West Mains and East Mains. These farms can be identified by the field names which appear on 18th century maps and are still in use.

Inn at Blair

In a few hundred yards the Wade road leaves the modern road, which branches off to the right. The military road continues to follow the Park till it crosses Drummond Field, passes round St. Bride's church and reaches Tigh Glas, the inn at Blair, now the Factor's House. This appears in a 1504 charter as 'Le Ale House with croft in Le Kirktoun of Blare', in favour of John Stewart, son of John, Earl of Atholl. Extensive repairs were carried out to the inn in 1679; Colin Ross in East Mains being paid £78 Scots for his food and wages due for 'working and plenishing the whole inns of Blair with beds and boords sets, tabills partition walls and lofting of ye said house'. The accompanying account of £21.15.2 Scots for 'iron supplied', included 'single and double plenshons, window bands, locks for outer doors, window tacketts and door bands'. In 1725, Patrick Mackglashan, former tacksman of the Mill of Blair, was granted a nine-year lease of the inn or change-house. His rent was:

	Scots		
	£	s	d
For the Inn	13	6	8
For malt kiln and barn	10	0	0
For the ward	12	0	0
For a crue lamb	1	0	0
	£36	6	8

He was also obliged, as casualties, to provide 10½ bolls each of meal and bere, 24 poultry, lead 50 loads of peat and make no charge for preparing the Duke's malt. Further improvements were made in 1736 when Patrick Mackglashan paid nearly £900 Scots 'for boxing, plastering and furnishing the new changehouse in Blair', made up as follows:

	£	s	d
		Scots	
Deals and Backs	217	1	10
Peats and wages burning two lime kilns for plaister	37	10	0
Carrying lime from the Kiln to Blair	3	0	0
22 stone of plaister hair at 12/- each	13	4	0
4 stone Spanish whitening at 14/- each	2	16	0
2 pecks screws at 6/- each		12	0
3,500 blind flooring nails	12	5	0
1,000 double plenshons and 1,000 single	6	0	0
1,200 nails	18	0	0
350 inch spriggs	9	0	0
10lb glue	3	5	0
Harling rooms before plaister	2	8	0
17 ribbes for chimneys for 17 rooms	7	0	0
Kitchen grate	13	11	0
Thomas Clark, Mason	62	5	0
Harling the house	96	0	0
Harling the house	8	0	0
John Lawder		16	0
	£512	13	10

	£	s	d
1. Donald Robertson, 10 days work about the house at 6/- day for coasting and draining	3	0	0
Andrew Macmillan, slater	3	4	0
2. Alexander Beck, glazier	10	4	0
3. Robert Thompson, John Wyllie, wrights	219	3	2
4. John Anderson, Smith	37	8	0
Candles @ 4½d per pound	1	16	0
Robert Low, Smith at Blair	2	8	0
	£277	3	2
	£789	17	0

1. Donald Robertson in East Mains for digging a ditch to drain the water whereby the Change House is miserably over-run with under water.

	£	s	d
2. 2½ doz. pean glass at 6/-		15	0
½ doz.		2	0
		17	0
3. John Wyllie, 75 days at 12/- day	45	6	0
Robert Thompson, 86 days at 12/- day	51	12	0

4. Includes shillen bands, door bands, locks for chamber door, door snaiks.

Major alterations were carried out in 1736, when the inn was completely rebuilt and enlarged to include at least 17 rooms. Patrick Mackglashan was given an allowance to employ tradesmen to 'build the new house of Blair and a sufficient stable, repair the malt barn and to lay out the expenses in the frugalyst manner' and by then his rent had escalated to £230.3.4 Scots. The new stable held 26 horses, 8 more than the one it replaced and to the east of the inn there was a stable for his own horses and a byre. The barn which adjoined his garden was pulled down and the stones used to build his garden wall. In 1744 a brew-house was built at one end of the stable 'in which was a Copper properly sett. The two coolers to go the full length of the House, the top of the first cooler not to exceed 5 foot that it may be even with the bottom of the Copper. The second cooler to be one foot lower and to go a foot under the first. Each cooler to be 10 or 12 inches deep'. In 1760 Patrick Mackglashan was paying a rental of £24.9.0 Sterling for:

'the inn, malt barn, stables and other houses in Kirktoun of Blair, bounded on the south by the street called the Market Place, west by street called Minigaig Street, to the north end of the malt barn, and on the north from the north end of the malt barn in a straight line to the wall that encloses Bellaloan and from there in a straight line to the road side at the east end of the stables, together with the garden betwixt the Market Place and the Church Yeard as the same as walled in as also the land that is inclosed by the stane and lime wall of Bellaloan on the east end by the dry stane wall that joins Bellaloan wall at Ginn Corner and runs from thence up to the foot of the hill and from thence West till it joins His Grace's inclosure by the side of the glen'.

Tibby's Lodge in 1860 with Mrs Forbes at her spinning-wheel. The arch was built across the military road in 1755 and it and the lodge were demolished in 1884 when the East Lodge was built opposite, beside the entrance to Glen Tilt.

In 1771 the lease of the inn was advertised and no offers received. This surprised the factor, situated 'as it is on so public and well frequented a road'. Later that year a proposal was submitted by John Stewart, brother of Donald Stewart in nearby Blairuachdar, butler and clerk of the kitchen to the Earl of Morton for the past ten years. The factor observed that he might do very well, 'even suppose he is a Highland man.' He was marrying an English girl, 'ideal for keeping a Public House as she had very good skill of cooking and house-keeping'. If his proposal was approved, John Stewart planned to go to London to purchase furniture, feather beds, blankets, chairs and tables 'which are much cheaper and better than in Scotland'. He did insist however that the inn should be repaired as it was 'not fit to accommodate gentlemen'. These repairs included harling the outside of the house, repairing the roof, 'sack and plaister the North-most garrett for accomodating gentlemen's servants to sleep in', installing dressers in the kitchen, repairing windows and jambs and tops of chimneys. He also asked the Duke to stop all tippling houses in Blair from selling spirits and ale, as he would always have sufficient stocks to meet the demand from villagers and travellers. In 1772 he was granted a year's lease and this included a shieling called Ruidh Riabhach in Glen Bruar and pasture at Urrard Beg west of the castle. Here he was permitted to keep three cows, essential 'for accommodating lodgers and travellers with fresh butter and cream'. John Stewart was still the landlord in 1795 when he asked for a rent reduction and assistance with repairing the inn. The factor indicated there could be no reduction and there was no obligation by the estate to undertake any repairs as he was making a handsome profit from the inn and also from the corn mill which, because of a plentiful supply of water from the Tilt was fully operative when other mills had ceased working due to frost. In the face of all this opposition John Stewart became worried about losing his job, and according to the factor, 'had been completely cured of the disease of asking down the rent.'

Around this time Robert Heron stayed at the inn and was greeted by a 'snug room, a blazing fire, a warm supper, some well-mixed rum punch and the kind attention of the landlord and landlady which soon refreshed me after the wetness and fatigue of my journey from Dunkeld. That I might the sooner enjoy the benefit of the fire, I was invited into the family parlour', he tells us. Dorothy Wordsworth was another guest a few years later and when she arrived at the inn at 10 p.m. found the place in uproar because of a fair held nearby that day. But she was 'civilly treated and was glad, after eating a morsel of cold beef, to retire to bed'. Elizabeth Grant of Rothiemurchus was a regular visitor and 'was accustomed to a particularly good pudding, a regular souflée that would have done credit to a first rate French cook, only he would have been amazed at the quantity of whisky poured over it'. She described the inn at Blair as being 'high up on the hill, overlooking the park, the wall of which was just opposite the windows'.

At the turn of the century, Robert Robertson from Tummel Bridge became the landlord and stayed till 1814 when he was removed because of his implication with others in a plot to kill deer illegally. His place was taken by John Cameron of the Nile Tavern, Perth, who was well recommended for the job. He applied to the estate in 1820 for a loan of £100-£130 to build an additional stable and post-chaise accommodation since a regular coach run between Perth and Inverness had been established and offered to pay interest of 7½%. By 1821 his widow, who had been running the inn during his long illness, was anxious to continue and was recommended by her father and brother-in-law, both men of good character and means, who guaranteed her ability to manage the place satisfactorily. The factor knew her to be 'a cautious, prudent woman, gentle in her manners, attentive to her own business and with superior education'. On 23th June 1830 the 4th Duke laid the foundation stone for a 'new inn' to be built at the Haugh of Blair and in 1832 the former inn, Tigh Glas in Old Blair, was closed.

Old Blair

The village of Old Blair, formerly Blair Atholl till by-passed in the 1820s, appears in a 1504 charter as 'le Kirktoun of Blare, a merkland.' In 1665, the rental of the village, which included Marjorie Kirkwood's croft nearby, was £7.6.8 Scots plus 21 bolls of meal and malt, 60 poultry and 60 loads of peat from the moss. In 1679 Thomas Conacher, wright from Tulliemet was paid £6.13.4 Scots, as nine days' wages for himself and an assistant, for making a 'Cobble to ye kill of Blair' and an extra £3.3.0 for food and drink. The lime kiln was located near Hercules Walk and the quarry to supply it, south of the Castle Loch. The village provided 11 men for the Duke of Atholl's Fencibles in 1705 and 1706, and in 1760 the Blair community included Robert Robertson, merchant; Lauchlan McLauchlan, shoemaker; Robert Anderson, smith; Donald Robertson, schoolmaster and Donald Donaldson, wright. Donald Donaldson had lived in the village for seven years serving 'most gentlemen between Logyrate and Dalnacardoch'. He married a Miss Spinks who had remained in the family house after her father had departed, till the housekeeper, Mrs Bradshaw 'was suitably provided'. When the time came for her departure, Donald came with a horse and cart and being unable to alert Mrs Bradshaw, removed his wife's belongings and chest through a downstairs window. At this moment, Mrs Bradshaw 'appeared in a passion' and although the contents of the chest were shown to her, she remained unconvinced. Donald

Donaldson begged the Duke's pardon for his rashness as he felt that 'leaving in this manner had laid the girl open to suspicion of theft'. Daniel Defoe toured the area in 1769 and describes what he saw: 'The town (Blair) consists of only a few peat houses, except the minister's house, one pretty good change or Public House and a poor old kirk'.

With the coming of the military road in 1728, the main approach to the castle was from the north-east, where a tree-lined avenue left the highway near the gardener's cottage at the corner of Hercules Park, passing through Stuart Field to the castle. This was the route that Richard Pococke would have taken in 1760 and in front of him he would have seen three knolls. He described a 'pleasant summer house that commands a fine view of the whole. On the middle hill is an urn; on the other to the East is an obelisk with a gilt ball on the top round which there are seats which I believe will be removed'. The summer house was called the Octagon, an eight-sided building completed in 1751, the same year that the Urn, sometimes called the Vase, a decorative cornucopia, was built on the adjacent knoll. Both the Octagon and Urn were pulled down in the last century and no traces remain today. The obelisk is situated on Tom na Croiche and is called the Hangman's Tower, old name Balvenie Pillar. This marks the last public hanging in Atholl which took place in 1630. Two foresters, Stewart of Auchgobhal and MacIntosh of Dail Fheannach, both in Glen Tilt, spent the night in a bothy in Glen Fender with their ghillie after a day's shooting on Beinn a' Ghlo. In the middle of the night Stewart stabbed both men with his skean-dhu and put one body on top of the other, hoping it would be assumed that they had killed each other. But the ghillie had not died and managed to summon help. When Stewart learned of this he fled to Sutherland, a place well-known in those days for harbouring criminals. But the Earl of Atholl was determined to bring Stewart to justice and sent a man named McAdie disguised as a beggar, who knew Stewart well, to seek him out. Eventually he found him and a body of Atholl men was dispatched to Sutherland to bring back the murderer dead or alive. This they did and the obelisk was built by Duke James in 1755 on the spot where the execution took place.

Old Blair in 1913 showing the estate Factor's House, formerly 'Tigh Glas', the inn, with stables to the right. This view has changed little in 75 years except that the trees have been felled. Old Blair was 'Blair Town' until the road was re-routed in the 1820s.

New Route

The military road from Tibby's Lodge to the inn only lasted for 24 years as in 1752 the public road was diverted further north. Starting from the inn, the new road went in an easterly direction through an avenue of beech trees and passed a lodge built at the back of the Octagon, subsequently pulled down by the 6th Duke in the last century. The line of trees is still visible, crossing the modern road and forming the southern boundary of the Bailanloan field, where the old highway passed the Toldamh curling pond, constructed in 1758, and near the Balvenie Arch. This stone arch over the highway was part of a walk formed from the castle to a summer-house built on the west bank of the Tilt, to provide a magnificent view of the Falls of Fender. All through the Tom na Croiche planting, the road is clear as it winds its way through the trees to come out in the field above the East Lodge, its direction still marked here by three trees, before rejoining the military road. A hundred years later, a new road known as the Post Road was constructed to Old Blair, equidistant between the military road and its successor and is the one we use today.

The military road passed in front of the inn at Old Blair and crossed the *Strabhaig* (little Strath), a small stream flowing from Blairuachdar, by means of a bridge built in 1755 at the southern end of Minigaig Street. The dry arch was built in the same year to connect the manse situated near the road, with the nursery opposite called Smith's Croft. From here it is a steep descent to the Banvie Bridge, rebuilt by General Wade After Diana's Grove, the road, at this point tree-lined and with a wall on each side, went straight on through a field gate and the line is clearly visible between pairs of trees where it crossed the Broom Know. Another obelisk stands on top of this knoll, built in 1742 at a cost of £16 to commemorate the family association with the Isle of Man. A year later it was demolished during a savage storm but was rebuilt.

A settlement called *Ardindeor* (height of the thicket) 864 666 was formerly located between the military road and the Whim. Mentioned in 1505 as 'Ardinaewry', the tenant in 1665, Donald McNeill Stewart was paying a rent of £5 Scots with 18 bolls of meal and malt at £5 a boll, 18 poultry and 80 loads of peat delivered to Blair Castle. In 1739 the land was enclosed and formed part of the castle policies and became known as High Park and Low Park. Cult More and Cult Beg are two more settlements which were thrown into the policies in 1739 and were situated north of the road. *Cult More* (big nook) 854 663, features as Mekil Quylt in a 1504 charter and was a two merk land in 1725 containing four tenants. Alex Gow and Donald Murray had a 9-year lease on a 10 shilling land and paid £24 Scots per annum, 30 loads of peat and were responsible for maintaining the dyke between the waters of the Garry and Banvie. Likewise Donald Gow possessed a 10 shilling land, paying similar rent, while James McMillan leased a 40 penny land, paying £8 and 10 loads of peat. The remaining 40 penny land of this two merk area had already been enclosed by the Duke and included within the policies. *Cult Beg* (little nook) 857 662 was a three merk land and in 1683 the tenant, Robert Stewart, loaned 800 merks to John, 1st Marquis of Atholl. Because of this the rent was reduced to £8 Scots per annum and he was freed from paying any casualties and services. The road descended the brae at *Crom Raon* (bent meadow), where a settlement of the same name provided two men for the Fencibles in 1705 and 1706, crossed the Deer Park and joined the public road opposite the Black Island, so called because in the 18th century there were some islands in the Garry.

Urrard

A settlement called *Urrard More* 849 660 was located here till 1739. It is first mentioned in a 1451 charter as being a detached part of the Barony of Lude, granted to Alex Reid of Straloch in 1498. It was acquired by John, 5th Earl of Atholl in 1589 in exchange for Pitnacree, located above Lude House. There were three tenants farming here in 1735, Finlay Stewart with a merk land and paying £42 Scots a year and 30 loads of peat, and George Ritchie and Donald Stewart, each with a half merk land and each paying £25 Scots and 15 loads of peat yearly. Within half a mile, and just before the railway bridge, the road reaches *Woodend* 845 659. In 1798, there were eight tenants paying between them a total of £26.1.0 and the following year they were called before the Baron Bailie for 'destroying growing timber'. They pleaded guilty to taking wood for fuel because the winter had been so harsh and were told they would have to leave their holdings in consequence. The tenants pleaded with the Duke to reverse his decision as they 'are happy under His Grace's wings and wish to stay'. Further problems arose the next year when six of the tenants petitioned the Duke as their families were starving and they were in 'the most alarming straits'. Although they had money, because of an acute shortage of bere and oats, they could not obtain even a peck and pleaded with the Duke to supply them with meal to keep their families alive. Donald McBeath, tenant in 1815, was caught stealing timber for his house which was in such a bad state of repair that the roof collapsed. He maintained he was felling old decaying trees which he intended to use for repairs. The case was heard by a Perthshire J.P. and he was fined £7.5.0 for illegal woodcutting. By 1820 there was one tenant here, John Stewart, who paid £50 for Woodend, Black Isle and Boat of Invervack – the Woodend Ferry. It was observed in that year that John Stewart was £25 in arrears and being the ground officer for the area, would have it deducted from his salary. The Woodend Ferry was an important link on the road from Tummelside, past Loch Bhac and Invervack to Blair. A new ferry boat was built in 1769, Neil Stewart, boatman borrowing £7 at 7½%. Nothing remains of the ferry today, save for the name of a field south of the Garry – The Bell Park – where a bell for summoning the ferryman at Woodend was located.

The settlement of *Urrard Beg* 842 660, sometimes known as Wester Urrard, lay west of Woodend. Donald Stewart lived here in 1723 and being in charge of the nearby woods, asked for ten merks as two years' wages. His crops had been poor and he was in debt to John Cowan who 'rests not night and day craving for payment and threatening to poind all he has'. Donald Stewart told the Duke he had nothing left to pay off his creditors or to purchase the necessities for maintaining himself, his wife and 'numerous babes'. The Duke promptly made him a payment of ten merks for keeping the woods. By 1735 there were three tenants farming here each with a seven-year lease and paying between them for this 3 merk land, £120 Scots, 20 loads of peat and 20 poultry.

West of Woodend all traces of the road have been obliterated by the railway, but in the garden of the West Lodge, there are the remains of an old bridge 13 feet in width. It is in a dilapidated state and very overgrown with saplings and undergrowth but probably formed part of the road at this point. The West Lodge was built in 1867 by the Highland Railway Company within four years of the Perth – Inverness railway being opened. Here the military road joins the modern road for a straight run of about a mile to Bruar. The old manse lies a few hundred yards north of the road at this point. For some years it had been thought that a manse located in the centre of the parish and equidistant between Blair and Struan would be of great benefit to the minister and enable him to cover his vast parish more easily. A contract was therefore prepared between the Duke and the Rev. Alex Stewart to build ' a new manse between February 1750 and August next and also walls and dykes of a proper and convenient garden'. Five honest sworn men thought that the 40 shilling land of Easter Baluain, with its shieling at Ruidh Dorcha Mhor, would equal the Glebe of Blair with its shieling at Allt Sheicheachan. It was agreed that the minister should retain a room in the manse, or

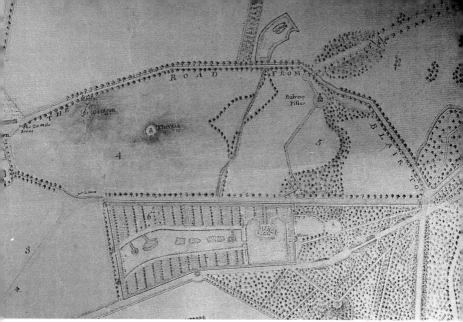

This 1758 'Plan of Atholl House, Gardens Parks and Inclosures' by James Dorret shows the route taken by the military road approaching the church from the east and passing Hercules Park. Within 24 years the direction had changed with the new road going due east from 'Blair Town' through an avenue of trees. The Balvenie Pillar marks the spot where in 1630 the last Atholl public hanging took place.

in the school shortly to be built in Blair, to which he could retire on Sundays and sermon days. After the scheme for building a new church in the centre of the parish was opposed in the 1820s by the Robertsons of Struan, Lude, Auchleeks, Kindrochet and Blairfettie, the manse was enlarged and in 1826 new offices were built at a cost of £150 and the house completed two years later for £578.

Baluain

The settlement of *Baluain* (lamb town) 833 661 is divided into two parts, Easter and Wester, and lies just north of the railway. It is reached by an arch under the railway at the back of the old manse farm, leading to two cottages. It appears in a 1669 Charter as 'Beluaine' with the tenants leasing the shieling in Glen Bruar called Ruidhchlachrie and in 1671, in a Crown Charter, for Blair Castle and 'Bollowaine'. By 1706 it was supplying ten men to the Fencibles and in 1725 there were five tenants here:

Land	Tenant	Tack	Rent Scots £ s d	Services	Peats
½ merk	John Stewart Mc. Cuilt	11 years	12 0 0	½ wedder	20 loads
½ merk	Jean Stewart	11 years	12 0 0		
½ merk	John Gow	11 years	12 0 0		
10/-	John Stewart	11 years	18 0 0	¾ wedder	30 loads
10/-	Donald Stewart	11 years	18 0 0	¾ wedder	30 loads

Wester Baluain, a few hundred yards along the track, was feued to Duncan Robertson of Auchleeks at the turn of the 18th century and in 1736 he sold the feu which included the use of two shielings, Ruidh Dorcha Beg and *Ruidh an Eachdraidh* (sheiling of the story) to Patrick Mackglashan, the Duke finally buying back the feu in 1772. Many families continued to live in the Baluains throughout the 19th century and only 60 years ago, there were two double dwellings, measuring 48 feet by 10 feet and two single houses, one thatched and one corrugated, still inhabited.

Examination of the records of the Parish Poor Fund at the start of the last century throws revealing light on the conditions of a number of people living in Baluain at that time. Isabella Cameron, aged 87 and widow of John Shaw, lived here alone in 1820. She had spent most of her life in Atholl and was deserted by her husband soon after they were married. She had one son whose whereabouts were not known and according to the parish assessment, had an excellent character and received 9/- a month out of the Poor Fund. Jean Fergusson, aged 69, and her sister Catherine a few years younger, were daughters of a crofter and both worked in the fields with increasing difficulty but they did not feel happy when idle. They were described as being 'quiet, industrious, sober, honest women, very kind to their neighbours'. Catherine Hay aged 58 years, unmarried daughter of a weaver had spent all her life in Baluain, 20 years of which she worked on an estate farm. She had an excellent character and was grateful for a little assistance from the Parish Poor Fund in winter when she had no regular work. Elizabeth Robertson aged 50 and her younger sister Betsy, daughters of a labourer, had resided in Atholl all their lives. Elizabeth had for many years been employed on an estate farm, but Betsy, because of a deformed arm, had never been able to work. They lived together and were thankful for any assistance the Fund could give them in winter as there was no field work available. Finally, Mary Gordon, a 50-year old widow, a native of Badenoch had been a resident for 22 years. Her husband was an old man in his dotage when she married him and he died many years before, leaving her with a son and three daughters. Mary 'has never quite been sane and has gradually been getting weaker in intellect. Now she is not responsible for her deeds, some of which are not always lawful', the report concluded. Her son was an apprentice and seemed to be doing well, and her oldest daughter was in service. Her second was very unsettled, like Mary, and the youngest was cared for by a stepsister, daughter of old Gordon by a previous marriage. Mary received 4/8d. a month from the Parish.

A track leaves the back of Easter Baluain and after half a mile, reaches Upper Baluain, now obliterated by trees. This became known as *Bee Jock's Croft* 832 664 named after John Robertson who lived there with his widowed mother in 1870, when he reclaimed the land and built a cottage. By a special arrangement with the Minister, the Rev. Dr. Irvine, he paid a rental of £3.10.0 for this croft until his death ten years later, when it was leased to different tenants. By the end of the century, it was described as 'that wretched house' by the minister because it was virtually uninhabitable and the value of the land greatly decreased through lack of cultivation. It was portrayed as a common lodging house and the minister was anxious to remove the tenants and pass the feu back to the Duke. However, 'Common humanity and Christian neighbourhood forbid my disturbing the MacIntoshes where poor Johnnie is dying' wrote the minister. 'My idea is to leave them till November. There will be no eviction'.

CHAPTER 5

Calbruar to Auchlany

The Military Road

Calbruar was situated a few hundred yards west of Wester Baluain and marked the start of the Brae Lands of Faskally. A charter of 1504 mentions the following as being part of the Brae Lands: 'Lands of Callvine, Callybruar, with its pertinents and Pettagowan'. It also included settlements extending as far as Dalnamein on the north side of the Garry. The Robertsons of Faskally were a branch of the Struan family and the Brae Lands were sold to the Duke of Atholl, for £4,353.3.4 in 1767.

There is no trace today of *Calbruar* (wood of Bruar) 828 662, though at the turn of the century it consisted of two double houses, thatched and in good order. In 1751 there were three tenants living there, Duncan McFarlane, Alex MacIntosh and John Cameron who each paid a rent of £20 Scots, 3 quarts of butter and cheese, (conversion £2.10.0) and a lamb value 13/4d, making a total of £23.3.4. By 1767, the first year under the Atholl Estate, rents had increased to £3 Sterling for each tenant, who also had to provide 40 loads of peat for the castle fires. By 1790 there were four tenants paying a total of £20 rising to £24 in 1801, before rentals were amalgamated with Baluain. Christy MacDonald aged over 80 years, lived here at that time and at the end of her days was bedridden, destitute and in her dotage. She received 6/- a month from the parish and her neighbour Sandie Gow was quoted as being very kind to her, visiting her often. In 1857 there were 16 tenants living in Calbruar.

The next settlement, *Balnacroft* (croft town) 823 662 was closely linked with Calbruar for rental purposes. In 1819 the main tenant was the widow of Alex Gow, who paid £100 in rental together with 24 poultry and also had to make two deliveries of coal from Perth to Blair Castle. Also living with her was her son Donald, who was described as a worthless fellow, 'behaving in a very slippery way'. By 1822 she was £40 in arrears and the question of sequestration arose. An inventory of farm livestock and equipment revealed that there were four horses, six cows, five stirks, two calves, 80 sheep, four pigs, four carts, two ploughs and harrows, available to cover the debt. The house itself was in a 'very ruinous state' and the factor felt that if new tenants were to be found, it would need complete renovation. He maintained they were 'very backward and had conducted themselves very strangely regarding their renovations'. The reason for widow Gow's problem was one of economics, the farm not producing enough return to cover the rental. In 1822, it produced £91.11.6 from crops, arrived at as follows:

Crops	Acres	Bolls Sown	Bolls Return	Price per Boll	Total Amount £	s	d
Oats	6½	7	16	16/-	12	16	0
Barley	3¼	3½	15	18/-	13	10	0
Pease	1¼	1¼	3½	13/-	2	5	6
Turnips	¼			80/-acre	1	0	0
Potatoes	1½		60	6/-	18	0	0
Grass/Hay		lost	lost				
Grass for Pasture	2			20/-acre	2	0	0
Lint	½	lost	lost				
Subset	19		£34 £8		42	0	0
					£91	11	6

Thus her 34-acre farm was insufficient to cover her rent because her crop returns were poor. Oats showed a return of just over two to one, when, according to the estate, it should have been 3½ to 1 while barley, though better, produced a ratio of just above four to one, when it should have been five to one. Her income was supplemented by sheep, as in the spring she would buy in 50, fatten them during the summer and sell at a profit. But this particular year she had sold none. She also reared cattle to sell at a year old and so far had only managed to sell two for £3. Lachlan MacIntosh had lived here for 40 years, and was alarmed when he learnt the Duke was annoyed at the way he was keeping the woods at the Falls of Bruar. He insisted that sheep must have strayed into the woods at night and caused some damage but they had been chased out at

In the 19th century Balnacroft was a small hamlet consisting of several houses, barns and byres, with fields extending up the hill behind. Here beside the railway we see the last remaining house before it was burnt down in 1977.

daybreak. He said that when his small farm was taken away from him and added to the main farm in 1817 his only source of income came from maintaining the woods. In 1977 the one remaining house in Balnacroft was burnt down but Donald Dow the tenant was unhurt. The burnt-out remains can still be seen beside the railway.

Bruar

The military road crossed Bruar Water at a point a few yards higher up the river than the present bridge which was built in 1926 near the sites of the two Bruar mills, a meal mill and a lint mill, both situated below the road. An early mention of a bridge at this point appears in 1721 when the Justices of the Peace threw out an estimate for its construction because 'there is much of that money exhausted', and many other bridges had to be considered first. It was not till seven years later that Wade bridged the Bruar. The earliest reference to a meal mill at Bruar occurs in a 1504 charter, when it was the principal mill for the Brae Lands, all the settlements being thirled to it. Its rental in 1615 was £10 Scots and this included pasture land for two horses, four cows and 30 sheep. By 1767 the first year under the Atholl estate, the miller, Duncan Robertson was paying £23.15.0 rent plus 12 poultry, 20 loads of peat and three carriages of coal to Blair Castle, as services. He also paid £2 for the use of *Dalvagaldie* 822 686, a settlement a mile upstream. In 1790 a lint mill for processing flax was constructed below the meal mill and this was leased to George Robertson for an additional £8 in rent. By 1807, his widow was the main tenant and she employed John MacFarlane, a miller from Pitagowan where he also had a small farmstead. Widow Robertson was described as a 'deserving though unfortunate person' and was heavily in debt. At that time the farmhouse was extensively renovated, 7,000 slates were bought for £9.9.0, two carpenters were paid £20.9.0 for their work and James Scott was paid £3.17.9 for glass. Her rental for the mills and farm was £70 and returns were inadequate:

1823 Bruar mills and farm

	£	s	d
Farm produce	41	18	5
Multures	9	12	0
Lint mill	6	0	0
Sale of five cattle	10	0	0
	£67	10	5

The farm consisted of 20 acres of arable land on which oats, barley, pease, turnips, and lint were sown, with 6½ acres for hay and pasture. Multures were made up of oatmeal, £3.16.0; barley, £2.16.0 and malt, £3. By 1829 the tenants astricted to the mill were refusing to repair the croy at Bruar Water until they were given 'a mill fit for work' and in the same year, an interesting proposal was put forward for converting the lint mill into a distillery. According to the proposal, the neighbourhood lacked a market for its produce – many tenants had supplies of barley which they could not sell, and were tempted to turn to smuggling, with 'ruinous consequences'. The report continued 'There is always a plentiful supply of fine water from the Bruar, the road passes it and the fuel,

Clach na h-Iobairt (stone of sacrifice) stands across the road from the Clan Donnachaidh Museum which opened as a centre for the Clan in 1969. The Falls of Bruar Hotel, formerly a farm, is beside the Museum.

which is a material object to a distillery is not difficult to be had'. They suggested that as lint was declining in popularity and less and less of it was grown in the vicinity, any funds the Duke might be laying out on the mill, would be better used for a distillery where the still-house could be built in the walls of the lint mill. They therefore asked the Duke to grant a supply of timber for necessary building and a loan of £200, half to be paid off in instalments, and interest at 5% to be paid on the remainder. The scheme was rejected; by the mid 1830s both mills had ceased and the farmhouse converted into an inn.

Information about the inn is scarce. In 1846 Thomas Jack was paid for repairing the roof and harling the Bruar Inn and in the same year the new tenant William Burns would not take possession 'unless the place is made comfortable. Either do what is wanted, or let me do it', he told the estate. In 1852, Samuel Robertson, innkeeper was paid 13/- for supplying whisky to men at harvest time and supplied £2.11.6 worth of whisky to sheep shearers. It ceased being an inn in 1863 with the coming of the railway and reverted back to a farm, with

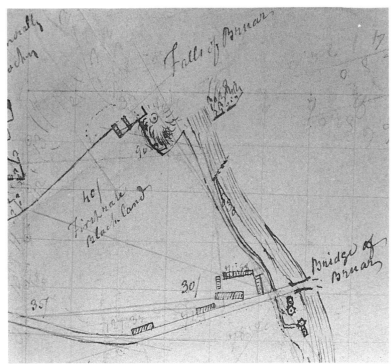

A traditional four-square farm at Bruar can be seen above the road in this 1790 plan. Below the bridge are the sites of the two water-powered mills. The one nearer the road was the corn mill for the Brae Lands of Faskally, with the lint mill below. Further up, the mill lade can be seen leaving the river.

Samuel Robertson continuing the tenancy. Exactly 100 years later in 1963 it once again became an inn, and is now the Falls of Bruar Hotel. Upstream are the famous Falls of Bruar, immortalised by Robert Burns who spent two days in Atholl in September 1787 and afterwards wrote his Humble Petition of Bruar Water. Verse five seems to capture the sentiment of the poet:

> Would then my noble lord pleases
> To grant my highest wishes
> He'll shade the banks wi' tow'ring trees,
> And bonnie spreading bushes.

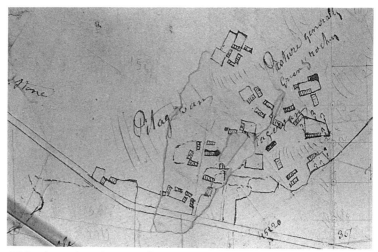

This 1790 plan shows Pitagowan with up to 40 houses, barns, byres and about a dozen enclosures. The military road is seen in the plan, passing below the settlement.

> Delighted doubly, then my lord
> You'll wander on my banks
> And listen many a grateful bird
> Return you tuneful thanks.

At the time of his visit Bruar Falls were awe-inspiring but barren because of the lack of trees and shrubs on the banks. It was not until 12 years later on the death of the poet, an event which must have troubled the Duke's conscience, that trees and shrubs were planted. The *Bruar Toll Bar* 822 659 was located a few hundred yards west of the inn on a bend in the road. This closed in 1879 and reopened in 1886 as a post office until the start of the Great War when it became a private dwelling-house, which was eventually demolished in the 1950s. *Clach na h-Iobairt* (stone of sacrifice) is located across the old A9 from the Clan Donnachaidh Museum. In 1792 there was one large stone standing with two or three round it to form a circle.

Pitagowan

Pitagowan (smith's portion) also part of the Brae Lands and the next settlement along the road, was acquired by the 3rd Duke in 1767. A 1615 charter by Duncan Robertson of Faskally granted the 'sunny half of Pittigowne' extending to a 40 shilling land, to William McConneill Mic Innes and by the year of the acquisition there were seven tenancies here, paying £16.1.8 in rent, 9 poultry and 190 loads of peat. This had risen to 12 tenancies in 1816. An analysis of 11 of these tenants, their farms and the factor's comments, makes an interesting study of the make-up of a settlement in the early part of the last century in the Highlands.

PITAGOWAN PENDICLES 1822
One year leases

Tenant	Rent			Farm Acres	Crops Sown	Return		
	£	s	d			£	s	d
John Robertson	15	10	0	8¾	oats, barley, turnips, potatoes, lint	19	9	0
Mrs McDermid	4	0	0	1¼	oats, barley, pease, potatoes	2	18	3
Alex Stewart Alex Gow	18	0	0	8	oats, barley, pease, turnips, potatoes	22	19	0
John McFarlane	5	15	0	2¼	oats, barley, pease, turnips, potatoes	6	15	6
Widow John Ferguson	10	0	0	1¾	oats, barley, pease turnips, potatoes	5	17	3
Angus Robertson	10	0	0	4¼	oats, barley, pease, turnips, potatoes	10	6	6
John Stewart	5	5	0	2½	oats, barley, pease, potatoes	5	10	0
William Robertson	5	5	0	2¼	oats, barley, turnips, potatoes	5	19	0
Duncan McLauchlan	5	5	0	3	oats, barley, pease, potatoes	5	13	3
Donald McFarlane	5	5	0	2½	oats, barley, potatoes, lint	5	14	0
John Robertson	4	4	0	1½	oats, barley, turnips, potatoes	4	10	0

Factor's Comments

John Robertson	Rather a good tenant but entered to the farm in bad order.
Mrs McDermid	Was allowed £9 for building a house in 1814.
A. Stewart A. Gow	Bad tenants, labourers but lazy.
John McFarlane	Miller to Mrs Robertson at Bruar from whom he receives wages.
Widow John Ferguson	A decent tenant.
Angus Robertson	A flax-dresser and well employed.

Pitagowan as a clachan in 1860 is typical of many hamlets in the Highlands which consisted of scattered houses and barns. The houses in the foreground were built in the middle of the 18th century with stone and lime walls. The heather thatching was secured by a number of horizontal slats. The wooden gable-ends have been roughly flattened at the top to be nailed on to a beam while the bottom end rests on a rubble base.

John Stewart	A flax-dresser and dyke builder – well employed.
William Robertson	A very bad subject, labourer well employed.
Duncan McLauchlan	A sheriff messenger and a useful fellow.
Donald McFarlane	A labourer and able to work.
John Robertson	Very infirm and not able to work – was formerly a carrier.

Pitagowan Cottars 1822

Cottar	*Lease*	*Rent*		
		£	s	d
Alex Cameron	1 year	1	0	0
Alex Robertson	1 year	1	0	0
Donald McDonald	1 year		6	8
Margaret McIntosh	1 year		6	8
		£2	13	4

Paupers paying no rent, each with 1 year lease:
Lauchlan McIntosh, Widow Seaton, Widow Duff, Christian Stewart Grizel Gow, Janet Robertson, Janet and Christian McIntosh.

Calvine in 1900 showing a row of houses beside the old A9. The Post Office was in the building on the right and beside it is the start of the track to Glen Bruar and the Lodge.

The land was fertile round the farms, that to the north described in 1800 as being 'pasture, generally green and rocky,' while between the village and Bruar Water it was first rate black land and across the road to the south, 'good arable.' As with other settlements, a number of the inhabitants of Pitagowan in the 19th century received parochial aid whilst others never asked for it. William Stewart aged 80 was a widower whose family was out of the country and gave him no assistance. He was described as 'a man whose habits are most industrious and he works as much as he can, a most deserving character who has never asked for aid'. Widow MacDonald aged about 80, married an old pensioner who did not survive the marriage for long. Since his death she had lead a most industrious life 'though delicate and feeble'. Her father had a croft at Pitagowan and for many years was a carter between Edinburgh and Blair Atholl. She received 8/- a month from the Parish and was described as 'highly respectable' by those who knew her. Widow Gow, aged 91 years, spent all her life in the same house. She had been bedridden for six years and was supported by a son who was a messenger in a jeweller's shop in Edinburgh. Her only daughter, Janet, lived with her and looked after her all the time as she could not even turn over in

81

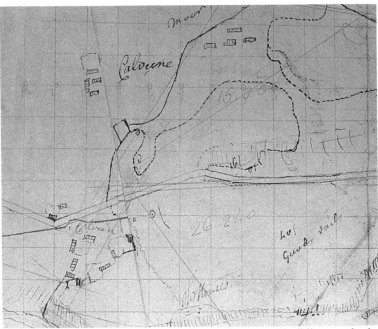

This 1790 plan shows Calvine, made up of scattered buildings on both
sides of the road built in the 1770s when the military road was
re-routed at this point.

bed. Widow Stewart spent all her 57 years in Atholl and
had one son who was not quite sane and worked on the Calvine
Farm. She supported herself by knitting stockings and received
no aid. David Barclay was an old Irishman with no family and a
wife who appeared contented. He acquired the rights of a
resident whilst employed in breaking stones and hawking tea
and although he received 10/- a month from the Parochial
Board, it was thought he was not as destitute as he made out.
George Robertson, over 70 years old, was blind and lived
with Donald Stewart, a contractor. George had spent all his life
working as a ploughman and agricultural labourer and
although he received 12/- a month in aid, he sometimes begged
from visitors to the Bruar Falls.

In 1773 the Wade road between Pitagowan and Crom
Bhruthaich went out of use as an easier line of road was built
nearer the Garry. The Wade road takes a sweep to the right

immediately after Pitagowan and evidence of this can be seen at the railway where a low passage was built to accommodate the track. As it climbs the hill, all traces of the road have been obliterated and it was near here that there was, until the coming of the railway in 1863 another settlement called *Sheneval* (old town) 812 658, its location being in the line of the track. In 1767 there were two tenants here, John Cameron and Peter Ferguson who each paid £3.15.0 rent and three poultry. Three years later they had started to enclose their land, borrowing £16 for building dykes at 7½% from the estate, resulting in £1.4.0 being added to their rents. Its population in 1823 was 14 people, by which time it had been included in the Calvine rentals.

Calvine
In 1753 Calvine, a five merk land, had five tenancies as follows:

	Scots		
	£	s	d
Tenant Duncan Robertson, rent	26	13	4
A stone of cheese a quart of butter or	3	6	8
1 lamb or a merk		13	4
	£30	13	4
Duncan Stewart/Duncan Robertson, same	30	13	4
Donald McFarlane/John McMillan, same	30	13	4
Ewan McColl/John Robertson	22	13	4
Duncan Robertson/John Forbes	44	13	4
	£159	6	8

In 1823 it had a population of 66 including four weavers, one midwife, a shoemaker and a wheelwright and boasted a grocer's shop. That same year, Allan and Alex Stewart were paying a rental of £350 for Calvine Farm and were in arrears to the sum of £169.2.8. Plans to sequestrate the holding were made by the factor after he had ascertained the farm stocks which were: 200 wedders, 500 ewes, 500 hoggs, 400 lambs, 44 head of cattle together with six horses, carts and

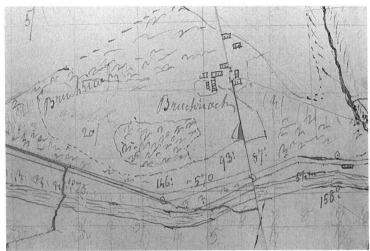

In 1790 Bruochriach consisted of 11 buildings and enclosures and all traces were completely obliterated when the new A9 was built in the 1980s.

three ploughs. The factor, Fred Graham,, was having trouble with another two of his Calvine tenants, Alex Robertson and Donald Robertson. Having received the demand for an immediate settlement of the £20 they were in arrears, they claimed that the dyke they had built for the estate at the county march would easily cover that sum. But the factor insisted on payment within seven days and his comment about their attitude was that they 'seem prepared and ready for anything but not paying the money'. In 1899 because the railway line was doubled, Calvine Farm was moved back and completely rebuilt.

Once above Calvine, the military road is clearly visible as it strikes diagonally across the ridge and is a pleasant 2½ mile walk till it drops down to the new A9 highway. A mile on from Calvine the road descends steeply to cross Allt a' Chrombaidh by means of a spectacular military bridge called *Drochaid na h-Uinneige* (window bridge) 791 668. Until recently this bridge was in need of urgent repair with one of the stone buttresses in danger of collapse but in 1985, a team provided by the Association for the Protection of Rural Scotland undertook a

A fine example of a Wade bridge called Drochaid na h-Uinneige which crosses Allt a' Chrombaidh east of Old Clunes and is part of a well-preserved 2½ mile stretch till the track descends to the new A9. This bridge was extensively and sympathetically restored a few years ago.

major rebuilding programme and the bridge has been excellently restored to its former glory. At *Clunes* (pasture) 784 673 the old settlement north of the shooting lodge, the road is lost for several hundred yards but is picked up easily on the other side.

In 1802 a number of tenants in nearby settlements petitioned the Duke about the Clunes tenant, William Stewart, who was impounding their cattle. They maintained they had tried to be good neighbours by returning any of his beasts that had strayed on to their land but Stewart would not return theirs without a payment being made. At the same time, he refused to pay for any of his stray cattle. In 1820 Bill McMillan was paying a rental of £320 a year for Clunes and the Tomnasallen pasture nearby and his arrears totalled £279.6.6 of which £160 was in dispute. He was described as a 'very difficult person to deal with', maintaining he had paid the £160 in 1816, for which he had not been given a receipt, and could produce witnesses to prove it. The factor decided to confiscate his holding as quickly as possible to prevent him from removing his stock. The shooting lodge at Clunes was built in 1867 and extensions made the following year.

The military road maintains its directness as it clings to the 1,000 feet contour and reaches the bridge over *Allt nan Cuinneag* (stream of the pail) 781 678 another bridge which has recently been repaired by the A.P.R.S. *Tomnasallen* (knoll of salt) 783 680 is located upstream on the east bank and with the nearby settlement of Craig contained at least 30 buildings and several enclosures. A large green lay to the north of the village and beyond there was an area described as 'good hill pasture mixed with green old shiellings'. In 1802 James Stobie the factor produced plans to rationalise the farms in the area and part of his programme was to amalgamate Clunes and Tomnasallen into a large sheep run. This would contain 1,429 acres made up as follows:

Inclosed by head dyke	98 acres
Muir inclosed by head dyke	31 acres
Open hill	1,300 acres
	1,429 acres

In place of the old combined rent of £23 (Clunes £17, Tomnasallen £6), he was offered £60 by William Stewart, 'a substantial and good tenant'. The settlement of *Bruochriach* (brindled bank) 778 675 was located a few hundred yards downstream on the west bank, and has been completely obliterated by the construction of the new A9. This comprised 13 buildings, a kiln and several enclosures. In 1772 the land here was enclosed, the tenant being advanced £2 at 7½% interest to build dykes, an extra 3/- appearing in his rental for that and subsequent years. In 1805, two tenants of long standing, Alex Robertson and John McFarlane were warned to leave their farmsteads because they 'countenance those who go about and are called by name, missionaries'. This they admitted, insisting they were not against the king, or government. 'They seek nothing but instructing us in the way of God more perfectly, wishing that we should leave of sinning and turn unto God', they wrote in defence of their actions. Their pleas were accepted and six years later Alex was

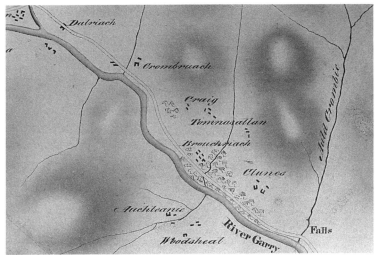

This detail from 'North West Perthshire' by J Douglas in 1821 shows the re-routed military road crossing 'Auld Crombie' and passing through six more settlements in the Brae Lands of Faskally before reaching the 'Lochgarry' estate at Dalnamein.

petitioning the Duke concerning fences. He said that his arable land had been enclosed by a wooden fence when the new road was put through lower down towards the Garry, to replace the Wade road in the last century. He maintained he would have to give up his farm land unless a dyke was built on the north side of the road from the Clunes march to his farm, where the land was 'good dry pasture'. The settlement called *Craig* (crag) 777 685 is situated south of the ridge of Tom Buidhe na Craig and is divided into two parts, surrounded by a 'dry green pasture'.

At this point the military road begins its descent towards the Garry and until recent road building obliterated the track, it was in excellent condition. A few hundred yards of it are visible again across the old A9 where it is very overgrown with heather, as it reaches *Allt Crom Bhruthaich* (stream of crooked bank). Nothing remains of the Wade bridge across this stream although the approach road and buttress were visible till the mid 1970s. The Highland Commission built a replacement bridge in the 1820s a few hundred yards to the south. This bridge remains and is a single stone arch which was the only

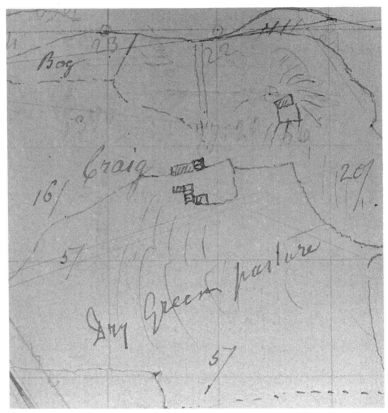

Craig comprised at least 12 buildings and was divided into two parts. The west section is shown in 1790 and was home 25 years earlier to Marjory and Joan Robertson who had a seven-year lease, paid £5 Sterling a year in rent along with 60 loads of peat to the laird's residence and 3 long carriages (haulage of wood and coal).

bridge not altered during the major road works in the 1920s. The settlement called *Crom Bhruthaich* 770 688 was located north of the military road on the east bank of the stream and although there is no trace of it now, orginally it was situated on a small plateau and contained buildings and enclosures in an area of green pasture. Again, construction of the new road in the 1820s caused concern to tenants. The new bridge here caused £6 worth of damage to Peter Stewart's land as 400 yards of dyke enclosing part of the haugh land had been taken down.

A few years later, Crom Bruthaich was described as a 'wretched place' being occupied by beggars who were replaced by Alex McIntosh, 'a substantial man' from Bruochriach. Stobie's plans for these three farms involved reorganisation rather than amalgamation. Each was in single occupation and each was allocated pasture and arable land, with a share of hill grazing:

Settlement	*Acres within head dyke*	*Acres arable*	*Old rent*	*New rent*		
			£	£	s	d
Craig	57	13	8	17	0	0
Bruochriach	46	14	8	17	0	0
Crom Bruthaich	20	5.5	4	6	10	0
	123	32.5	£20	£40	10	0

There were 123 acres of ground enclosed within dykes and 1,000 acres of hill pasture for the three farms.

Immediately across the stream the military road rejoins the old A9 and runs with it, with minor deviations, as far as Dalnacardoch. The settlement of *Dalriach* (brindled haugh) falls into two parts about half a mile apart and beside the military road. There is no trace of *Easter Dalriach* but *Wester* 761 693 is still inhabited as a holiday home and an interesting feature is the bench-mark set in the wall of the building. Donald Robertson was the tenant here, paying a rent of £6.6.0 when he died in debt in 1785 leaving his wife Janet MacDonald to run the small-holding. Brother Angus took pity on his sister and helped her to run the farm and bring up her children, eventually settling there. In 1787 Janet obtained a lease for half a plough of land for 14 years and Angus commenced improving the farm by enclosing it with dykes, building farm houses, converting waste land into arable ground, all at his own expense. To his astonishment, in June 1797 Janet 'executed a summons of removing' against him resulting in his being turned out, as she was proposing to give the farm to her son, a young unmarried lad in service.

Finally, the last settlement which was included in the Brae Lands of Faskally was called *Mealdoulash* (black grey hill) 761 705 situated a mile to the north, at the 1,500 feet contour level, in open countryside and sometimes known as Little Dalnamein. There are substantial remains of 13 buildings, two kilns and enclosures, representing the two farms that made up this settlement. Once again Stobie's plans for the four farms in Dalriach and Mealdoulash involved re-organisation rather than amalgamation. Although he would have preferred a large sheep run, the location of these farms prohibited this and as the tenants were all 'good people', their boundaries were redrawn and they shared the hill pasture:

Settlement	Acres within Dykes	Old Rent £ s d	New Rent £ s d
Mealdoulash			
West Division	9		9 0 0
East Division	9.5	8 8 0	9 10 0
			£18 10 0
Wester Dalriach	7		8 0 0
Easter Dalriach	9.5	6 6 0	5 10 0
			£13 10 0

Area contained by dykes was arable/pasture
Hill pasture attached to farms: 900 acres

Woodsheal and Auchlany

Across the Garry from Clunes Lodge and outside the Brae Lands is the settlement of *Woodsheal* 775 668 which consisted of 14 buildings, a kiln and several enclosures. Up to 1752 this formed part of the Robertson of Struan estate, when because the family was implicated in the 1745 rebellion, it was annexed by the Crown until 1784 when it was restored to Colonel Alex Robertson. The Duke of Atholl arranged for the land to be surveyed by John Lesslie in 1758 and he reported that it contained 20 acres and provided potential for improvement:

	Woodsheal	
A deep wettish soil, very improveable	9 acres	
A light free soil on a sandy base	5 acres	
A morass very improveable by draining	6 acres	

In 1826 The Duke of Atholl bought Woodsheal, together with

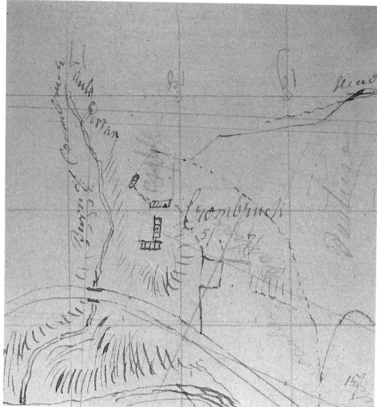

Crom Bruthaich, shown in 1790 as a small farmstead of 4 buildings beside the burn after which it was named. It has completely disappeared under the new A9.

Auchanruidh and Cuiltaloskin in Glen Errochty from Robertson of Struan's trustees, for £6,387.

The fertile settlement of *Auchlany* (field of the enclosure) 773 670 lies next to Woodsheal and being Atholl property surrounded by Robertson land, the boundary between the two places was established in 1730 when a 'deposition of several old men' fixed it on the stream flowing between them. The remains are substantial consisting of several buildings to gable-end height at the south end of a large area of pasture. Auchlany was leased to the Robertson family of Blairfettie from over the hill in Glen Errochty throughout the 18th century but by 1802 it was falling into a bad state of repair and the land had been neglected. One of the tenants came from Rannoch and being an 'idle fellow' was removed and his place taken by a man from Tomnasallen. In 1805 Thomas McDonald obtained the tenancy and he reported it was in 'bad order, buildings uninhabitable so much that it would be expensive to put them right'. By 1815 when the rent had risen to £30, Thomas died and the tenancy had been taken over by his widow. The factor's assessment in 1820 indicated that her son, considered an active lad, would be staying at home to manage the farm: 'Their means are not great but they have worked very well through a great arrears of rent', the report concluded. Widow McDonald was given a three-year lease in 1822 and was described as a 'very respectable tenant', who until the previous year had been hampered by subtenants. In that year she grew oats, barley, turnips and potatoes on 7 acres of arable ground and devoted 2½ acres to grass for hay. She supplemented her income by selling 17 stone of wool for £6 and pastured five tups and 90 ewes for £9.12.0. The route to the settlement is clearly defined by a ford across the Garry, the Auchlany Ford, and a well-made track leads right up to the dwelling houses, which were inhabited till well into the 20th century.

CHAPTER 6

Dalinturuaine to Drumochter

The Military Road

Across the Garry opposite Wester Dalriach lies the settlement of Dalinturuaine which marked the start of the 'Lochgarry' estate. This land, stretching to the County March appears in a 1451 charter as 'Terris de Glengere Cum Foresta, belonging to Roberto Duncanson de Strowane'. A Royal Charter under the Great Seal of King James V in 1513 granted the land to John, 2nd Earl of Atholl, when superiority of the land was removed from William Robertson of Struan who had defaulted in payment of a debt of £1,592 Scots to the Earl. In 1738 James, 2nd Duke sold the feu rights for £1,356 Scots to Donald MacDonnell of Sandwick who immediately assumed the title 'Lochgarry'. In 1746 the estate was annexed to the Crown and MacDonnell accused of high treason 'for his being engaged in the late un-natural and wicked rebellion' and in 1788 the feu rights were repurchased by the Duke of Atholl for £4,800 from Lieutenant Colonel John MacDonnell, son of the original feuar.

In 1772 the estate was surveyed by William Tennoch as a prelude to the Duke buying back the feu rights from the Crown.

SURVEY BY WILLIAM TENNOCH 1772

Settlement	Arable	Improveable	Moor	Moss	Total Acres
Dalnacardoch	19	21	637	41	718
Dalnamein	20	31	890	32	973
Dalinturuaine	25	15	766	57	863
Tomicaldonich	4	6	836	33	879
Dalinriach	8	11	1,255	77	1,351
Commonty of Dalnacardoch	—	—	30	140	170
Commonty of Dalnamein	—	—	607	203	810
Total	76	84	5,021	583	5,764

Settlement	Present Rent			New Rent		
	£	s	d	£	s	d
Dalnacardoch	16	13	4	31	10	0
Dalnamein	13	6	7	23	8	0
Dalinturuaine	10	0	0	17	16	0
Tomicaldonich	5	11	1	10	10	0
Dalinriach	5	0	0	19	0	0
Total	£50	11	0	£102	4	0

His report concluded:

'These farms have a right to a share of the high hill grazings at Loch Garry where the pasture is very good from the beginning of June to the middle or end of September. Upon the high grazing their cattle are greatly refreshed with the young verdure which has not been touched for the preceeding nine months, while their lower pasture grounds adjacent to their farms are greatly hained during the summer months that their cattle were feeding some miles distant.'

In 1794, 14 tenants from the estate petitioned the Duke about the high rents charged by the late Colonel MacDonnell. The severity of the previous two seasons had resulted in the loss of most of their stock they maintained and as their ground produced no lint or grain equivalent to that grown elsewhere they had no means of paying their present rent. The factor's comment was that they had suffered in common with other tenants by recent crop failures and 'their muir soil is improper for the culture of lime'. At this time, Stobie was planning to convert the area to sheep, as this report shows:

'This district from its high situation with extent of hill will not be beneficial to make one large farm. Many people lived there and a partial removal of some would not solve the problem unless those left behind work together on the present system at little additional cost to that of working the little specks now held by so many'.

At this time there were six tenants at Dalnamein, six at Dalinturuaine, and three at Tomicaldonich.

Dalinturuaine

In 1632 the lease of *Dalinturuaine* (haugh of rumbling stream) 759 691 was renewed for Charles Robertson of Auchleeks

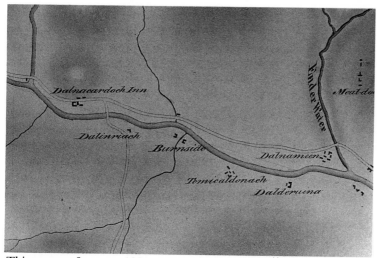

This extract from an 1821 map by Douglas shows the military road entering the 'Lochgarry' Estate at the 'Ender Water' and passing six settlements, these being Dalinturuainie, Dalnamein, Tomicaldonich, Burnside (East Dalinriach), Dalinriach (West Dalinriach) and Dalnacardoch where the inn was situated.

because it had been possessed by Robertson's ancestors, 'kindly tenants' and Atholl did not wish to remove them. He therefore granted a life rent, 'land to be laboured and manned, with pasture rights in the Forest of Glengarry'. By 1711 Donald Robertson was paying a yearly rent of 200 merks Scots, 3 stone of cheese and three quarts of butter. The 1772 survey shows that the tenants had little chance of increasing their arable land for corn as there was no more flat land on the farms. 'The hill ground is covered with heather interspersed with grass in several places full of large stones. It lyes much from the sun and greatly exposed to the northerly storms especially along the brow of the hill facing the Garry Water'.

In 1797 trouble erupted amongst the Dalinturuaine tenants. Two widows, Christian Stewart with six children and Rachael Cameron with seven complained that Donald Cameron rather than acting as a good neighbour to them in their time of need, took the opportunity 'at all times to harrass, beat, bruise and destroy them'. The widows took the matter so seriously they intended to, 'lay him under surety of lawburrows and receive damages for injury and loss sustained'. Later, more tenants petitioned the Duke about the behaviour of Donald Cameron and his wife. They claimed the Cameron dog had chased their sheep resulting in the loss of some lambs, and their neighbours had been assaulted. The Camerons had then threatened violence if they failed to sign a petition clearing them and by plying cottars with drink, had prevailed upon some to sign. One of the widows' sons was struck by a stone on his thigh which made him lame at harvest time. Trouble erupted again in 1813 when Ewan Cameron claimed that Donald Cameron's horses strayed during the night and destroyed his (Ewan's) corn. He caught them, shut them up in his barn and refused to release them till the damage had been paid for. At this Donald became incensed and threatened 'to lay his boot on Ewan's neck' and promptly broke down the barn door. In 1818 Donald accused Ewan and his wife of being bad neighbours. He charged them with stealing his horses at night and injuring them. Their children, under orders from their mother, had chased his cows over rocks and through his arable ground, organised cottars from Badenoch to abuse them with a 'bad tongue', and Ewan's wife was seen stealing hay out of their barn, her tracks in the snow having revealed her identity. Finally, in 1819, Ewan Cameron applied to the Justice of the Peace for redress and was granted a warrant against him to 'keep the peace' but Donald defied the court constables sent to take him to court and since then Ewan and his family had gone 'in fear of their lives'. Ewan could prove that Donald Cameron junior was a 'professed poacher' though he was unwilling to turn informer. He asked that Donald Cameron and his family be removed forthwith and he would be willing to take over their holdings and renounce his own, rather than continue as at present. In 1819 the factor reported that the tenants were a mischievous set of people, constantly thieving and fighting and many were evicted in that year when the farms were let to Duncan Robertson, described as a 'very timorous person, not very punctual with his rent but means well'. An example of this occurred in 1822 when Duncan owed the estate £40. The factor hoped he would have been 'honourable to his promise in paying up his whole arrears'. On being threatened with

Dalnamein shooting lodge in 1900.

> The stags they roam in plenty
> O'er the distant hills so green,
> And our host he looks for twenty
> As the kill at Dalnamein.
>
> With Gow and Jock and Jimmie,
> And a cavalcade not mean,
> They sally forth to battle
> From the Lodge at Dalnamein.
>
> When the day is wet and dreary
> And the stags are few and far between
> We hasten back, tho' tired still cheery
> To the smoking-room at Dalnamein. (1920)

(Charlie Gow was head keeper at the Lodge; Jimmy Menzies his underkeeper and Jock Campbell was the handyman and gardener.).

liquidation Duncan asserted he 'now hears of friends he can without any scruple pledge himself upon for paying the full balance of his due'.

Dalnamein

A few hundred yards before Allt Anndier, as the old A9 carries straight on, the military road branches off to the right and crosses the river by the Dalnamein Bridge, repaired in the 1820s and not by-passed till 100 years later. *Dalnamein* (haugh of the mine) 753 695 is south of the road at the point where it rejoins the old A9. The original settlement was located in a field east of the lodge where the footings of at least 14 buildings can be seen in the ground. There were eight tenants here in 1746 paying a total of £159.19.4 Scots in rent. A new house was built in the village in 1711, 44 feet long, 7 feet high and 14 feet wide and nearby tenants carried as much stone, mortar and timber as was required. In 1802 Stobie divided the Dalnamein area into small pendicles paying a collective rent of £22 along with a large farm on the west side with a rent of £30 making a total of £52, £18 more than the old rent. All the tenants accepted this division except for Stewart in Tomnasallen who was taking the Auchlany tenancy. In July 1819 Christian Stewart, a tenant, pleaded with the factor to be allowed to remain in her house, promising to 'flit' at Whit 1820. On that day she had an ejection warrant executed against her and everything she possessed was removed. She promised not to harbour or lodge 'any unbecoming person such as smugglers or poachers again'. The factor relented out of charity for the girl and gave her leave to stay.

During the early part of the last century, extensive building and repairs were carried out at Dalnamein, as the following entries show:

	£	s	d
December 1804			
Paid William Gow for building dyke	9	16	0
Paid McFarlane and Robertson for grubbing trees		18	9
Paid Robertson and Scott, sawiers	5	19	8
Paid McEwan and Taylor for 7,000 slates	8	1	0
January 1805			
Paid Jas. McNeil for building Dalnameen House (Probably the Lodge)	38	0	0
April 1805			
Paid Alex Cameron for carriage of slates by John McIntyre	4	5	0

July 1805
Paid Walter Dow for slating
Dalnameen House   4   16   6
Paid McDonald and Robertson
sawiers for Dalnameen House   9   4   2

November 1805
Paid Robertson for building
barn at Dalnameen   19   18   8

December 1805
Paid Alex McLaren for
wrightwork at Dalnameen
House   5   1   8

November 1807
Paid McIntosh and Butter,
sawiers for Dalnameen kitchen   3   2   2½
Paid Alex McLaren for
wrightwork of Dalnameen barn   9   12   11
Paid William Robertson for
building Dalnameen kitchen   14   9   0

November 1808
Paid William McEwan for
9,000 slates   13   10   0

March 1809
Paid Stewart Jack for slating   3   0   0

December 1811
Paid Dan Clark for slating
houses   13   14   9

1850
Mason work for gamekeeper's
cottage   14   0   0
Carpenter work for making
two beds   6   8   0

When discussing the area with the Duke, Stobie told him that
the land was now well let and as the rents no longer included
shielings, the rise would not be as great as elsewhere. He
indicated that Robertson of Kindrochet had offered £60 for
the whole but had withdrawn his offer when he realised the
number of families it would cast out. He said that few of the

Dalnacardoch Lodge in 1900, right beside the old A9. The wooden plaque to the right of the front door is a permanent reminder of the inn. The traditional outbuildings are to the rear. The inn closed in 1865 with the coming of the railway and was converted to a shooting lodge.

'Dalnameiners' would accept his new division even though he offered to remove some of the bad people and replace them with people from other places. He had a low opinion of the people of Dalnamein, who took little heed of his instructions and continued to use the run-rig system of crop cultivation as their forefathers had done.

Tomicaldonich

Another settlement mentioned in the 1772 survey is *Tomicaldonich* (knoll of son of Duncan) 753 693, located south of the Garry on a green pasture, where the remains of several buildings can be seen. Tennoch's survey informs us that this settlement was bounded by the Garry to the north, lands of Auchleeks at the watershed to the south, east by the farms of Dalinturuaine and west by Dalinriach. 'It falls under the same description as the previous farm, there being little or no difference as to the quality of the soil whilst the cattle on both farms feed promiscuously without regard to any line of division', he reported. Three tenants living here in 1799 had trouble with their neighbour, Patrick Robertson, Dalnacardoch vintner who impounded their cattle found straying on to his pasture and removed fir from their land for use in his kitchen. When they complained about this he came over with a body of men carrying knives and threatened to 'cut the horses threats (throats) or their lifes'. Consequently they found it impossible to live with him as their neighbour and petitioned the Duke to enclose their land with a stone dyke to prevent further impounding of their livestock. Patrick's version of this incident was that the Tomicaldonich tenants were so careless about letting their livestock stray on to his land, eating his grass and corn and breaking down the enclosures, that up to the middle of June he had chased away 200 sheep and impounded a further 45. At this the Tomicaldonich tenants had 'threatened mischief'. Three days later Donald MacDonald alias Mannoch claimed them and although maintaining he could not afford any compensation, offered to return next day with security. That night someone 'was cunning enough to steal them' and Patrick found them next morning, grazing on a hillside. As he was about to repossess them, Mannoch appeared with 'a parcel of dogs' as his security!

In 1823 the settlements at Dalnamein, Dalinturuaine and Tomicaldonich were combined to form one large farm under the tenancy of Duncan Robertson who paid a rent of £194. Livestock pastured on the farm in that year included: bulls 1; cows 13; stots and stirks 8; calves 11; tups 16; ewes 220; 3-year wedders 50; hoggs 60; gimmers 210; lambs 250 (of which 80 were bought in). He also sold 100 stone of wool and put down 6 acres of oats, 2 acres of barley, an acre of turnips, 1¾ acres of potatoes and 22 acres of grass for hay. The return from his farm for that year was:

	£	s	d
Livestock sales	73	5	0
Sale of wool	30	0	0
Subset in Dalinturuaine	50	0	0
Farm produce	81	0	0
	£234	5	0

The Wade bridge over *Allt Geallaidh* (stream of the pledge) was rebuilt by the Commissioners and consisted of two stone arches with spans of 11 feet 6 inches and 13 feet 3 inches respectively. In 1837 it was described as being very dangerous and in need of urgent attention. The disused Glen Garry School is still standing and is situated west of the bridge. In 1884 there was 'scarcely the semblance of a school here, save for three months in the winter'.

Dalnacardoch

In half a mile the road reaches *Dalnacardoch* (haugh of the smithy) 721 703, an important junction on the route to the north. This is where the Perth-Inverness road meets the military road from Stirling and the south-west, which is the subject of the next chapter. Wade had his 'hutt' here from which he directed the construction of this section of the road and this became the forerunner to the inn. In 1732 Charles Robertson of Blairfettie obtained the contract to build an 'inn and offices' here at a cost not exceeding 1,200 merks (£800 Scots) and was granted a 19-year lease which included the farm, for an annual sum of £80 Scots and two wedders value £4. The most famous visit to the inn happened in 1745, when Bonnie Prince Charlie set up his headquarters there in August before his victorious march into England and stayed on 10th and 11th February during his retreat to Inverness the following year.

The Rev. Francis Gastrell, touring the Highlands in 1760 reported that the inn was so filthy that rather than dine there, his party sat down outside on a green bank and ate their lunch of ham, tongue, bread and cheese, whilst Henry Skinner, who stayed there a night in 1795 described it as 'the good inn of Dalnacardoch, another of the houses erected by the Government'. At the end of the 18th century, problems of travelling to the north in winter gave cause for concern and the landlord, Patrick Robertson wrote that 'the road between Dalnacardoch and Dalwhinnie is extremely dangerous to travellers in winter because of the snow which has often prevented them from continuing their journey for a very considerable time. Lives of many are lost when attempting to proceed'. He therefore offered to provide horses and men to keep the road open and to protect and guide those on foot. He

The Edendon Toll House in 1924. Initially this was a two-roomed wooden building where dues were collected from all who crossed the nearby bridge, except pedestrians. In 1879 it was bought by the Atholl estate. The Toll House and bridge have completely disappeared with the latest road building programme.

would do this by providing four men to walk to Dalwhinnie and back, twice a week. They would set off every Tuesday and Friday at 8 a.m. and return from Dalwhinnie at 1 p.m. the same day and would not be expected to risk their lives during violent snow storms. If his horse was used to clear a track for carriages, he would charge 1/- per mile and he also needed 18 spades, similar to those used for repairing the military road, to be replaced every ten years. But the estate was dissatisfied with Patrick Robertson, removed him from his post in 1802 and the following year he sued for damages for wrongful dismissal. As the factor commented: 'As if all the names of Robertson were inspired at once by the demon of litigation, that rascal at Dalnacardoch has issued a summons for £300 damages for being kept out of his possession'. He was replaced by James Stewart, followed in 1815 by Donald Stewart 'a good tenant and innkeeper', who immediately asked for extensive repairs to be undertaken as the inn was in a ruinous state. 'I can't install

my furniture for public or family use – Better do it now (June)
as it is the slackest time of the year', he wrote. Travellers at this
time had mixed views of the standards of the inn. Garnet in
1811 described the inn as being 'a very good one. From
Dalnacardoch we proceeded to Blair Atholl, a distant ten miles,
the first half of our journey was by no means interesting being
among lumpish hills, covered with heath, but when we arrived
within about five miles of Blair, the country began to assume
the appearance of cultivation', whilst a few years later, Larkin
said that the inn, 'like all those on this great thoroughfare, is
provided with all the accommodation that can reasonably be
required'. In 1812 Elizabeth Grant was travelling north and
mentioned, 'the dreary moors to Dalnacardoch, another loan
house with a very miserable steading about it, and a stone-
walled sheepfold near the road'.

   An early mention appears in a 1680 agreement when
'Dalnachardich' and nearby Dalinriach were feued to Alex
Robertson of Blairfettie for an annual payment of a 'sufficient
fatt wedder sheep'. By 1822 Donald Stewart was paying £160
for the farm and inn and examination of the accounts for that
year show how profitable it was:

	£	s	d
Sales of livestock	489	14	0
Wool	100	12	6
Park for passing drovers	25	0	0
Farm produce	97	13	0
Estimated value of inn now lower because of Inverness coach replacing chaises, gigs	50	0	0
	£762	19	6

Donald was described as a good tenant giving great satisfaction
as innkeeper and had improved four acres of ground below the
inn at a considerable expense to himself. Livestock carried on
the farm in that year was considerable: bulls 2; cows 13; stots
and stirks 62; queys 6; heifers 1; calves 6; tups 40; three-year-
old wedders 260; two-year-old wedders 450; ewes 640;
gimmers 160; dinmonts 560; lambs 440. 2,610 fleeces were sold
at 6/- stone and crops sown were: oats 7 acres; barley 4 acres;
turnips 2 acres; potatoes 3 acres, and grass for hay 16 acres.

The park for passing drovers which produced £25 in grass money, was called the Drove Stance and lay south of the inn, on the other side of the Garry, where 200 sheep could be grazed. Two years later Donald complained that the recent road realignment between the inn and the Edendon Toll had passed through his best winter pasture and he was seeking compensation. He asked for a dyke to be built from the toll bar to his stables on the upper side of the road to keep passing drovers off his grass. There was already a retaining wall built when the toll was opened 'as absolutely necessary for preventing the droves of sheep and cattle going a by road without paying; and the extra cost would be but a trifle'.

In 1849 the factor was making plans to combine the farms at Dalnacardoch and Dalnamein which together could pasture 1,000 sheep and 16 Highland cattle with the arable land of the two extending to 60 acres. In 1865 the inn was closed because much of the traffic had been diverted to the railway but there is a permanent reminder above the front door where a wooden plaque has the following inscription in Latin, English and Gaelic:

HOSPITIUM HOC
IN PUBLICUM COMMODUM
GEORGIUS III REX
CONSTRUI INSISTIT
AD. 1774
REST A LITTLE WHILE
GABHAIS FOIS CAL TAMHILL BHIG

In that year, the farm was valued at £977.8.0 made up as follows:

	£	s	d
6 work and posting horses	60	0	0
9 cross bred milk cows	50	1	0
5 calves and 1 pig	9	0	0
850 ewes, wedders, hoggs, blackfaced	637	10	0

£756 11   0

12 small stacks of oats and straw	27	0	0				
300 stones of meadow hay	6	5	0				
30 stones of turnips	10	10	0				
				£43	15	0	
Implements	50	0	0				
Furniture	127	2	0				
				£177	2	0	
				£977	8	0	

Nowadays Dalnacardoch is a shooting lodge and in recent years the farm attached to it had 300 ewes, 80 hoggs, 8 tups, 2 cows and 4 calves, together with 4½ acres of barley and 11 acres of grass for hay.

Edendon Toll

The *Edendon Toll* 715 707, taken down during recent road construction, was situated west of the bridge over the Edendon Water and was a wooden building consisting of two rooms, with loft above and a large garden extending to a third of an acre between the road and the Garry. It was bought by the estate in 1879, for £60. The bridge, which has also disappeared, was extensively repaired and strengthened by the Commission in the 19th century and rebuilt with a single span stone arch of 28 feet, 8 inches. The Edendon grazing, an extensive area of pasture which lies to the north of the road was leased to Stewart of Shierglas in 1669 for an annual payment of three wedders and he was granted permission to pasture lowland oxen there. John and Donald Stewart, tenants from Tulach in Garryside, had leased the pasture for four years at a rental of £65 per annum and in 1794 applied for a reduction because they had 'tried all the industrious methods possible but now find they can make no more than £50 yearly, owing partly to lowness of market'. Their request was granted. After the toll the Wade road climbed the ridge away to the right where it was visible as a causeway till obliterated in the 1970s and in less than half a mile crossed *Caochan na Bo Baine* (stream of the white cows) 712 708 and part of a buttress was all that

The Edendon Toll Bridge, built by General Wade in the 1720s, extensively repaired in the 1820s but was taken down in the early part of the 1980s.

remained of this bridge until recently. The road heads straight for the lower pasture of *Meall Nan Ruaig* (hill of the chase) where several watercourses, intact and in good order have preserved this part which is visible as a grass and heather-covered track between two banks, beneath electricity pylons.

Wade Stone

Shortly after, the military road rejoined the old A9 and left it again after a mile to reach the *Wade Stone* 692 718. Legend has it that Wade placed a guinea on the top and returned a year later to find it still there. Originally the stone was on the left of the military road, going north. Now it is on the left of the southbound carriageway of the new road, but more or less in its original position. Within a hundred yards the military road crossed a steep gorge formed by *Allt an Stalcair* (stream of the stalker) 691 718, which was the western boundary of the Edendon grazings. The bridge here, initially called Duroure Bridge after a Major Duroure, Wade's quartermaster, has disappeared. When it was built it was only 10 feet wide and the approaches for 100 yards on each side so steep, with a gradient of 1 in 14, that horses had to approach at full gallop to get up the other side and to add to the problem there was a sharp bend at one end. The 1837 Commissioner's report states that since the mail coaches started travelling that way at night the previous year, parapet walls had been damaged and this bridge was particularly dangerous. *Rienastalker* (stalker's shieling) is a few hundred yards upstream and is mentioned in a 1659 manuscript as being leased to Alex Stewart of Foss. In 1784 this shieling was given to Glen Tilt tenants who had lost theirs at the head of the glen when they were added to the deer forest. By this time it had been combined with another shieling called Aldvack, a mile further up the road. Aldvack, mentioned in the 1600 Pont manuscript, was leased to Calvine tenants in 1669 for 2 wedders a year and by 1742 was 'lying waste and lee'. In 1785 it was handed over to tenants of Dalginross as their shielings at the head of Glen Tilt had also been included in the newly-formed deer forest.

Garbrough

The Bohally Shielings, also known as the Garbrough, after *Allt Garbh Bhruaich* (stream of the rough slope), an extensive area of pasture south of the Garry, were described in the 18th century as having 'moss and poor pasture at the summit'. Today, opposite the confluence of the Edendon Water and the Garry, there is a solitary barn 717 705, formerly a dwelling-house, and the remains of several earlier bothies can be seen nearby. It was shared between tenants of Port of Grenich, Bruachbane and Bohally under feu, and with tenants of Dalcroy, part of the Atholl estate. The original feu rights drawn up in 1737 reserved 'always to our tenants of the merk land of Dalcroy, the privilege of shealing yearly in the said sheal of Garbrough, in conjunction and commonty with the tenants of the said three merk land of Bohalie'. The commonty was therefore divided according to the merks of the settlements, three-quarters for Bohally and one quarter for Dalcroy, but by the end of the century, the ratio had changed in Bohally's favour and the Duke's tenants only had a one-sixth part for grazing. In 1829 the Duke of Atholl was offered the Bohally share of the commonty from the feuar, Charles McDiarmid, for £2,015 being 31 years' rental at £65 per annum. On checking, the

The eight-foot high Wade Stone seen in 1924 stood on the left-hand side of the military road going north.

factor discovered the true rental value was £50 per annum, described the offer as a mere device for raising the price, and the offer was declined. Allt Garbh Bhruaich formed the southern flank of the shieling boundary and a mile upstream there was another shieling called *Refuirst* (shieling of the pipetune) 710 699. This was described as an old shieling in 1669 and was located on flat ground, west of the stream where there are substantial ruins with several more overgrown footings of bothies. In 1771 this area was described as being of 'gradual ascent and covered with long heath and some good grass'.

The military road rejoined the old A9 soon after crossing Allt an Stalcair and followed it for a mile before branching off to the left, down towards the *Garry* 670 719. Why Wade built in this direction is not clear as, being so low-lying it was liable to severe flooding and indeed is still marshy, yet clear traces of the road remain at this point with stretches where the edging stones are still intact. By the 1770s the direction of the road had changed and again during the 1820s, to that of the old A9, when the Commission built a new bridge across *Allt a'Bhathaich* 668 721 with an 18 feet span. Until recently, remains of a buttress forming part of the Wade bridge could be seen a few yards upstream.

The *Coire Leathanaidh Shielings* (corrie of the meadow) 673 716 were located opposite, on a large expanse of hillside where there are some 20 rectangular footings in the ground, whilst another three are to be found at the confluence of the stream with the Garry, with a ford leading to an isolated bothy ruin. In 1669 there were three parts to this shieling called Rieninnair, Riestronnahitich and Riedie and it is possible to see the three divisions from the layout of the bothies. A few hundred yards west of Allt a'Bhathaich, the military road crosses a streamlet by means of a small stone *Wade bridge* 667 722, still remarkably intact despite its sinking foundations and in a short while crossed another stream, *Allt Chaorach Beag* (little sheep stream) 657 728 by means of a stone arch described in 1924 as an 'old arch on the Wade road, near mile 49'. No trace of this bridge remains but a photograph taken in 1924 has preserved it for posterity. Allt Chaorach Mor throughout its whole length from source to Garry formed the boundary between the Lochgarry tenants in Dalnaspidal and the Atholl tenants in Aldvack, whilst the land between this stream and Allt Coire Mhic-sith was little more than a commonty for these tenants. After buying the feu rights in 1738, Donald MacDonnell erected 37 new shieling bothies on both sides of the road across the face of Craig Chaorach and drovers with their cattle rested here at night, between the two streams. These shielings were tenanted by people from the Struan estate who were moved out of Dalnaspidal when the laird reorganised the land and raised crops. Milk cows were pastured on the hill above the shielings and returned to the bothies at night, while yeld cattle were grazed further afield and stayed all summer. Tenants were anxious to keep their yeld cattle on higher ground to prevent them becoming mixed up with passing droves. Likewise they were at pains to preserve the greens around their bothies and appointed a poindler to prevent cattle and sheep from straying on to their lush pasture. By 1787 the bothies were in ruins and in that year the Atholl tenants took over the pasture, drove off the Lochgarry cattle, planted 6 bolls of oats and 2 bolls of potatoes and grazed their own black cattle, sheep and horses on the land.

There are only the remains of a buttress of the Wade bridge across *Allt Coire Mhic-sith* (corrie of the fairy's son), known as Oxbridge, and replaced by a Commission bridge a few yards downstream in the 1820s. *Oxbridge* 646 736 was the site of a great feast in 1729 to celebrate the completion of the military road. Writing to the Lord Advocate, Wade mentions travelling from Ruthven:

> 'with great ease and pleasure to the feast of oxen which the Highwaymen had prepared for us opposite Loch Garry, where we found four roasting at the same time in great order and solemnity. We dined in a tent pitched for that purpose; the beef was excellent and after three hours stay took our leave of our benefactors the Highwaymen and arrived at the 'Hutt' (Dalnarcardoch) before it was dark.'

Dalnaspidal

An early reference to the *Dalnaspidal Shielings* (haugh of the hospice) 647 729 occurs in 1669 when they were leased to Robertson of Auchleeks for 'a fatt cow' or £16 Scots and remains of the shieling bothies can be seen in the ground a hundred yards east of the Lodge. In 1717 the tenancy belonged to Alex Robertson of Dalnacardoch and he paid 250 merks (£186.13.4 Scots) for the first three years and £200 for the remaining six years of his nine-year lease. For this he was allowed to pasture up to 400 lowland oxen each year. Cromwell is believed to have camped here during his punitive expedition to the Highlands and in 1745 General Cope drew up his army in expectation of an attack and finding none, continued his march northwards, thus opening the pass to the highlanders. After Donald MacDonnell had bought the feu rights in 1737, he built a house with stable and byre on the south side of the river, enclosed the meadows to raise crops and removed the shielings to different parts of the grazing. His house was burnt to the ground by government troops pursuing the retreating highlanders in 1746. In 1784 an advertisement appeared in a newspaper stating that the lands were 'extremely fit for grazing of sheep', a method of stocking which had not yet been introduced to that part and James Welsh, a farmer from

Roxburgh, took up at £100 a year, the 19-year lease: 'All and whole grazings of Dalinspiddle and Lochgarry, all within the said parishes of Blair Atholl and Strowan and that for the full and complete space of 19 years from and after Whit 1786'. He managed his farm in a most progressive way, ploughing up barren hillsides and attempting to grow corn where it had never been grown before.

The coming of the military road affected the Dalnaspidal community which saw opportunities to be gained from the passing traffic. Duncan Robertson from Tulloch had a bothy on the east side of the stream at the top of the green, stayed there all summer and kept a public house. He allowed drovers to rest their cattle on his shieling provided they paid for the pasture and the topmaster distributed bread, cheese and whisky to them from Duncan's bothy. Many travellers passed this way and in 1861 Queen Victoria described the scene: 'A little further on we came to Loch Garry which is very beautiful. There is a small shooting lodge or farm, charmingly situated looking up the glen. We passed many drovers without their flocks, returning from Falkirk.' Garnet in 1811 saw 'a lake into which two rivers emptied themselves. It was yet too soft to bear a considerable weight but was covered with a beautiful green turf, through which the river bent its serpentine course.' William Larkin in 1818 saw 'a broad verdant plain covered with short but remarkably fine and thick grass, with a handsome slate-roofed cottage apparently a hunting or shooting box, for which the situation is admirably adapted'. *Allt Dubhaig* (stream of the dark pool) 644 724 joins the Garry beside the Dalnaspidal Shielings. In 1812 John Campbell from Rannoch farmed the land to the west of the river while Donald Stewart of Dalnacardoch farmed to the east, with the river forming the boundary between the two farms. John Campbell's farm consisted of a fank, wool barn and shepherd's house with his hay meadow located close to the river, and his pasture on the lower slopes of the hillside. His rental was £40 Sterling and he farmed there for twenty-five years.

Drumochter

At this point we enter *Drumochter* (summit ridge), the great pass through the Grampians described by George and Peter

A lovely example of an old Wade arch near Dalnaspidal but now gone. This is typical of many of the bridges built in the 1720s and its simple construction ensured a long life. A coom of larch poles was built across the stream and stones carefully laid on it, the last being the keystone in the centre. The coom was then removed and the bridge became self-supporting, as the greater the pressure, the stronger it became.

Anderson in their 1843 Guide Book as, 'the bleak and moorish wilds where nought but stunted grass and heather, dark swamp, impetuous torrents, grey rocks and frowning heights and precipices are to be seen. The mountains also are heavy and seem to be broken into great detached mounds'. Earlier, Elizabeth Grant went through the 'high hill-pass' to Dalwhinnie. 'Nothing can exceed the dreariness of Drumochter', she wrote, 'all heather, bog, granite, and the stony beds of winter torrents, unrelieved by one single beauty of scenery, if we except a treeless lake with a shooting box on it'. William Larkin in 1818 saw, 'immense mountains, covered with heath, rising on each side and no human habitation in view except a Shepherds' Cottage, lately built and no spot of green herbage. An agreeable impression was conveyed by the comparative fertility of the dark mountains and moors of Drumnacher'.

The military road climbs out of Allt Coire Mhic-sith and here

113

it is a clearly-defined track through the heather. It crosses *Allt Ruidh nan Sgoilearan* (stream of the shieling of the scholars) 640 743 by a ford, and close to the shieling where the remains of circular bothies on the north side of the burn were evident. Duncan Robertson of Croftdow shieled here in 1737 and pastured his cattle further up the glen. *Allt Fuar Bheann* (stream of the cold mountain) was also crossed by a ford but earlier there was a bridge and old maps refer to this as the 'Bridge of Drumacter'. The nearby shieling 638 747 consisted of five bothies and was situated between the military road and the old A9. Atholl tenants started building shiel houses here in 1730 and Donald MacIntosh of Auchleeks shieled here for seven years, being the first man to build a bothy. By 1767 the shieling had fallen into disuse. The military road is still clearly visible in the heather as it heads straight for the County March. A chair stone was located at the top of the next ridge and below *Craig nan Ubhal* (rock of the apple). At this stone, which resembled a chair and had charcoal placed under it, several witnesses had their faces slapped and were sworn to the marches on bended bare knees. The chair stone was demolished when the military road was built.

At this point the road passes the eastern end of *Coire Dhomhain* (deep corrie). Coire Dhomhain and *Allt a' Chaorainn* (rowan stream) to the north-west of the road were the glens most prized by Atholl and Badenoch tenants who used them indiscriminately in the 18th century, along with passing drovers. Badenoch people claimed ground as far south as Dalnaspidal while Atholl folk maintained that the hummocks or *Sithean* (fairy knolls) around *An Torc* (the boar) were the march. In practice, thefore, there was a great deal of encroaching. Malcolm MacPherson of Crubenmore claimed he had seen the Atholl tenants taking cattle from the shielings of Allt an Creagach and An Torc and driving them to the south side of Coire Dhomhain. A scuffle ensued with Alex Robertson, a cousin of Blairfettie, and MacPherson told him that if it happened again he would be taken to Gordon Castle and imprisoned. The shieling at *Bruach nan Iomairean* (bank of the rigs) 602 748 was located on the northern slope of Coire Dhomhain and below the ridge at the junction with *Allt Fraoich* (stream of heather), in an area of rough pasture. Robertson of

Dalnaspidal shooting-lodge near Loch Garry where the remains of the original shieling are visible nearby. Dalnaspidal leapt into prominence after the military road was built, with an ale-house being opened, and drovers rested here with their livetock on their way to the trysts in the south, paying dues for their pasture.

Auchleeks built a shiel house here but his father pulled it down three days later. John McGregor had a bothy to the west of the shieling, when he was forester of the glen, and Duncan Robertson, who also pastured there, had eaten and drunk in this bothy at the end of the 18th century. The Atholl tenants, trying to establish the march at this point, would sometimes graze here without bothies, spending nights out in the open.

As the military road continues to the north it crosses Allt a'Chaorainn by means of a ford. The shieling here, which has disappeared, was located beside the stream and a few hundred yards from its confluence with Allt Dubhaig and Allt Coire Dhomhain. In 1730 John Duff from Dalnamein took over a house located to the south of the stream, which was established by the military when they were building the road the previous year and shieled here for two years with his cattle until he pulled it down. At the turn of the 18th century, Stewart, following his dismissal from Dalnacardoch, built a 'large whisky house' on the north side of the stream.

County March

The military road reaches the *County March* 632 760 along level ground where the toll bar started taking dues in 1821. John MacPherson, mail strapper (groom) lived at the march in 1851 but the coming of the railway changed the trade, and William Ross, platelayer in 1871 and Ronald MacDonald, rail surfacemen in 1891, were the new tenants. March stones marked the boundary between Atholl and Badenoch. Badenoch tenants maintained there were three stones opposite Allt Dubhaig and one of them stood in the course of the military road and was thrown aside during building. Other stones were located 200 yards south of *Allt an Creagach* (rocky little stream) with 'A' on one side and 'B' on the other. An 1819 charter document records a march stone between An Torc and the military road, standing in such a way 'that if you were to empty a pail of water upon the top of it, part of it would run to the County of Inverness and part of it to the County of Perth'.

For seven centuries, man has battled to build roads across the Grampians. First the Red Comyn who in the 13th century built the 'way of wane wheills' to take carts from Old Blair to Ruthven. Then, some time before the 17th century, the Minigaig Pass became the major way through and developed as a principal route for drovers. Wade established his network of military roads in the early part of the 18th century and these were repaired and re-routed by the Commission for Highland Roads and Bridges, a hundred years later. Finally we have the two major reconstructions of the 20th century to make way for the motor car. It is a fitting tribute to a great man that much of the new turnpike in Atholl is on the same line as his road of 250 years ago. Wade thus standardised the way through the Grampians that those using wheeled transport have used ever since.

CHAPTER 7

Dalnacardoch to Tummel Bridge

The Military Road

Even as he was completing the military road between Perth and Inverness in 1729, Wade was planning his work for the following summer and by the time of the feast of oxen in October, he had already carried out two surveys of the projected road from Dalnacardoch to Tummel Bridge and through to the south-west. This road which was only 12 feet wide, was an important addition as it connected the major military bases in Stirling and Glasgow with the network of routes covering the Highlands. By 1800 its principal use was as a drove road and local traffic was limited. Drovers had tended to take a more westerly route from the west coast by Fort William and Tyndrum but the failure of the bridge at the head of Loch Leven resulted in almost all the cattle and sheep from the north passing this way to the markets of Falkirk and Comrie. A vivid description of the conditon of the road in 1799 is given by a Perth lad, driving along in a chaise. He describes the journey as being:

> 'dreadfully hilly. All around me was a world of mountains with craggy tops and sides of sheep pasture, mixed with peat moss and heath. The road was firm and good but a constant up and down of long and steep hills, till I came in sight of a small valley, watered by the burn of Eroskie to which there was a descent by a very long zigzag. The village at the bottom is Trinefour, from which another laborious hill is to climb of above a mile, at the top of which is a terrible rough barren heath.'

In 1823 John Mitchell made a cursory survey of the road from Dalnacardoch with an estimate of the cost of its repair.

> *John Mitchell's report – 7th April 1823*
> *1.* From the bridge over the Garry to the first summit, altho' the line is not laid out in the most judicious direction, it is capable of being made a good road with a few slight improvements, such as raising the hollows to preserve the inclination, cutting off some ·

117

The Wade bridge called Drochaid Dail an Fhraoich across the Garry marks the start of the military road from Dalnacardoch to Tummel Bridge, Aberfeldy and beyond to the south-west. Little has changed since this picture was taken in 1924 except that there is considerably less water in the Garry now, and the bridge has been cemented.

awkward bends and this may be done at a moderate expense as proper materials are very convenient.

2. From thence to the Bridge of Glenerchie the present road is both too steep for wheel carriages and its surface in a miserable condition, being sunk under the surface of the adjoining ground, and its proximity to the hill makes it liable to lodge snow in winter, and is difficult and expensive to keep clear of water – In this distance of nearly three miles, the small materials are swept off, and the surface of the road presents the appearance of a deserted water course covered with large stones and rocks, and the expense of a complete repair would be little short of that of forming a new line in a better direction which when finished would be maintained at a moderate expense.

3. From Glenerchie to the summit of the next hill near Bohespic, the present line might be made a tolerable good road with some slight alterations at an ordinary expense, but from that point to Tummel Bridge the surface is in a wretched condition and completely covered with loose large stones and rocks. The repair here will be expensive, because the road is to be formed anew, and no material can be got but at great expense. The few cross drains which have been made in this and last five miles are all in a ruinous

A 19th century picture of Trinafour in Glen Errochty showing the sawmill, Wade bridge and Bridge Cottage on the right. These features remain to this day, though the mill shut down in the 1950s and the bridge is closed, even to pedestrians.

condition, and with the necessary side and back drains will of course inhance the expense.

Mitchell's report indicated that the road was in such a bad condition that a major rebuilding programme was necessary and the cost of the first five miles from Dalnacardoch he estimated to be £960 and for the next four, £864. In his calculations he allowed funds for building a toll house in Trinafour.

Dalinriach

The military road crosses the Garry below Dalnacardoch at a bridge called *Drochaid Dail an Fhraoich* (bridge of the haugh of heather) 726 700, a fine example of a Wade bridge built in 1730. The remains of a number of buildings can be seen in an area of flat green pasture beside the road. This was the settlement of *Dalinriach* (haugh of heather) 730 699 and in his 1772 survey, Tennoch indicated that 'spots of improveable land along the banks of the river (Garry) could be ploughed up,' to enable the rent to double. The coming of the railway necessitated the road taking a major deviation to cross it but

Trinafour House, formerly the inn on the military road. The wing on the left was added in the 1890s when the inn closed but it was demolished in the 1960s.

once up on the ridge the military road leaves the modern road at a bench-mark and cuts away to the left to cross *Allt Culaibh* (back stream) by means of the *Cowley Bridge* 728 689. Here the embankment and remains of a buttress can be clearly seen. This part of the road fell into disuse when the new route was completed to the west in 1827, forming a wide detour and crossing Allt Culaibh upstream. Charter Room records in Blair Castle show the presence of two shielings here, Couillia and Cuiilea both near the Wade bridge and the pasture was described as good. It was here that the lands of Atholl and Robertson of Auchleeks met and a boundary dispute arose between the two lairds in the early part of the 19th century. Atholl claimed the land up to the top of the ridge overlooking Glen Errochty while Auchleeks asserted his right to the pasture in common with the Duke, as far north as Allt Culaibh. The sheep in the area numbered 500, as many as the land could bear and Dalnacardoch and Dalinturuaine livestock were constantly moved off by the Auchleeks tenants. In August 1827 Robertson tenants removed 2,000 cart loads of peat from this land, leading the Atholl factor to comment that Auchleeks

The Glen Errochty Toll House in Trinafour beside the road to Tummel Bridge is the only one that has survived in Blair Atholl parish.

wanted to conserve his own peat mosses at the expense of Atholl's stocks. Lieutenant Duncan Robertson of Dalnamein had his peats broken as they lay drying, while Peter Robertson of Dalinturuaine, who had been cutting peats there for 20 years, had them thrown back in the moss by Auchleeks, but they were retrieved, dried and carted home. In 1829 the dispute was settled in favour of Auchleeks and Allt Culaibh established as the northern boundary of the commonty.

After crossing Allt Culaibh the Wade road survives as a heather-covered track between banks as it climbs steeply to rejoin the existing road at *Feith Mhorair* (lord's bog) 727 682. Here is the Wade bridge of Feavran, rebuilt by the Commission in 1827. About a mile upstream, across a flat marshy pasture, there is the ruin of a solitary bothy called the *Sheiling of Fevora* 714 674. This was built for Auchleeks around 1750 and shortly afterwards demolished by passing drovers. Auchleeks maintained it stood on his land and rebuilt it in 1826. 'The bothy at Fevorrah is nothing more than rebuilding of an old one which has always stood on the same spot', he wrote. 'This bothy was put up on my order last year to accommodate my

Trinafour Post Office, formerly Auchleeks Post Office, which stood across the road from the toll house. The wooden building on the left was taken down a few years ago when the Post Office closed.

people and belonged to my grandfather and great grandfather and has stood there from time immemorial,' he concluded. When the Atholl ground officer for the area, John Stewart challenged the building of the bothy, the Auchleeks overseer refused to take it down, declaring it to be outside Atholl property and promptly placed two men to keep possession of it.

Across the Bridge of Feavran the Wade road follows the modern road, passes close to *Maud Loch* 726 660, specially built as a trout loch, and descends into Glen Errochty by means of three hairpin bends. The track to Loch Chon leaves to the right at the first of these and within half a mile, passes the settlement of *Auchdruimahuagie* 722 655, where the remains of several buildings and enclosure walls are visible. This formed part of *Dalchalloch* (haugh of the kiln) 730 648, a settlement lower down the glen and in 1800 the tenant, William Stewart was pasturing his cows and horses on the other side of the hill at the Shieling of Fevora from the beginning of May to the end of October. His 21-year lease, for which he paid an annual rental of £73.10.0, permitted him to cast, win and lead peats from the west side of the military road and work and carry away limestone from the quarry on the other side of the Loch Chon track. In both places he was also allowed to demolish those houses and barns which he did not need for his farm at

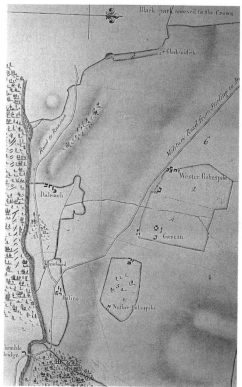

James Stobie's 1780 'Plan of Lands in Strath Tumble' shows the military road passing the six Bohespic settlements.

Dalchalloch, indicating that by 1800 the settlement of Auchdruimahuagie had become deserted.

Trinafour

The superiority of *Trinafour* (third of the pasture) 725 646 was acquired by John, 2nd Earl of Atholl in 1515 through a Crown Charter by James V following non-payment of a debt of £1,592 Scots owed him by William Robertson of Struan. A 1613 charter by William, Lord Murray granted to Alexander Robertson, described as a kindly tenant, 'all and whole the 40 shilling lands of Trinafour with houses, lofts, crofts, yards, shielings, grazings outsets and pertinents with the woods growing on the same, reserving full powers to the granter and

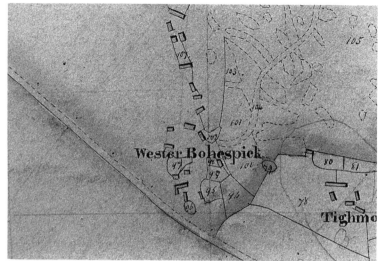

A detailed plan of Wester Bohespic in 1821 in which the 19 buildings that made up this settlement are seen. There were nine tenants living here at this time, paying a total of £51 in rent. The whole area of the Bohespics is now under trees planted after the last war.

tenants occupying the Mains of Blair to cut, intromet awaytake of the said woods'. The rental was 40/- Scots with an augmentation of £6 Scots making a total of £8 Scots which by 1665 had increased to £80 Scots and six stone of cheese and six quarts of butter. This sum included pasture rights of the shieling of *Sleoch* (mountain grass) 667 653 which until 1954 was used as a sheep fank until submerged by the dam at Loch Errochty. It was located at the west end of the loch, beside Allt Sleibh. The three merk land of Trinafour was leased to Patrick Robertson in 1727 for 100 merks and 16 loads of peat while the other half was possessed by Robert McArthur for £8 Scots and 16 loads likewise. The Errochty is crossed by a fine Wade bridge called the *Trinafour Bridge* 726 648 which was by-passed in the 1920s and is now so unsafe that even pedestrians are barred from using it. The Trinafour sawmill lies a few yards downstream, where a specially built weir fed the lade which conveyed sufficient water to power the wheel. The sawmill stopped working in the 1950s when completion of the Loch Errochty dam by the Hydro Board caused a considerable drop

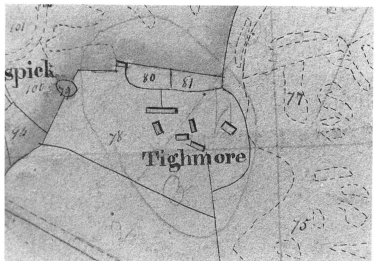

Tighmore, adjacent to Wester Bohespic contained six buildings as seen in this 1821 plan. A number of these can still be found amongst the trees with walls of two of them extant to 6 feet.

in volume of the water supply leaving only sufficient power to cut 40 fence posts a day.

Once across the Errochty the Wade road follows a grass track in front of Trinafour House, formerly an inn. Reference to an inn here appears in 1825, in a memo from Fred Graham, the Atholl factor. He reported that he had succeeded in removing John Stewart from Strathgroy 'in time to prevent the ruin of the farm and to put a stop in that neighbourhood to any further effects of his swindling propensities. He has shown himself utterly incorrigible which Mr Robertson will find out before Stewart has long been tenant of the Trienafour inn which he has taken.' The 1844 Statistical Account states that 'there is a good inn at Trinafour. Several small houses along the public road and at proper distances are licensed to sell spirits'. In Tales of Toll-Bars and Toll-Roads by the late, James Robertson of Rannoch, he writes of a notable Perthshire dame of 100 years ago, Dowager Lady Menzies, being a frequent traveller between Rannoch Lodge and the new railway station at Struan. One such journey progressed uneventfully until the inn. When the carriage arrived at the end of the loop in the

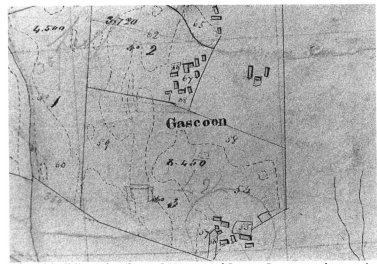

The 26 buildings that formed Upper and Lower Gascan can be seen in this 1821 plan. Gascan was the largest of the Bohespic settlements and is first recorded in a charter of 1621.

road, the horses headed straight for the inn as they usually did, much to the dismay of Duncan, the driver, who saw his credibility destoyed by a pair of horses. After much tugging and pulling he managed to direct them back to the road, shouting between each cut of his lash, 'you tam liars'. The inn closed at the end of the 19th century. As the road climbs out of the glen it passes the Glen Errochty Toll Bar, opposite the site of the Trinafour Post Office. This opened in 1846, was named Auchleeks Post Office in 1866 and was not renamed Trinafour until 1965, remaining a post office till 1985. Half a mile south of Trinafour, Robertson and Atholl lands met and this point is marked by a stone with 'A' engraved on one side and 'R' on the other. This was the northernmost point of the Atholl grazings of Bohespic where they marched with the Robertson land of Trinafour.

The Bohespics

The road is impressively straight as it climbs the ridge and, as it begins the long descent to Tummelside passes the Bohespic settlements on the left. A 1451 charter shows that Roberto

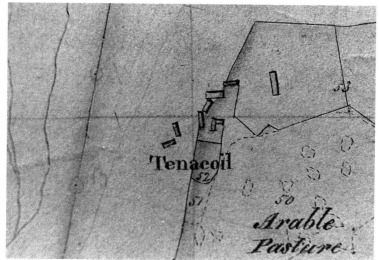

Tighnacoil in 1821 was a hamlet of 9 buildings, adjacent to Gascan. It first appeared as a separate rental in 1818.

Duncanson de Strowane was granted 'Terris de Duabus Bohaspikis', *Wester and Easter Bohespic* (Bishop's dwelling), which by 1515 when acquired by the Earl of Atholl, had become part of the Barony of Lude. A disposition in 1612 was granted in favour of Neil Stewart of Shierglas for the £8 land of Bohespic, providing 'he cut only so much of the wood as is necessary for beiting, mending uphauling of the houses and biggings of the same'. By 1621 the £8 land (12 merks) had been divided into a number of holdings, Wester Bohespic (4½ merks) and Gascan (2 merks), being leased by Neil Stewart's second son George for a wadsett of 2,000 merks, and the 1½ merk land of Dalriach. In 1642 the four merk land of Easter Bohespic was granted to Margaret Robertson, sister of Donald Robertson of Struan and in 1754 Dalriach, including Wester Bohespic, was granted by James, 2nd Duke to Lieutenant James Robertson, son and heir of the late Neil Robertson of Bohespic.

By 1801 James Stobie, Atholl factor had completed his reorganisation plans for the area and wrote: 'I have made a neat division of Bohespike in the hill as well as the arable farming, the whole into regular farms and taken offers from the best of the tenants which amounts to about £260, £40 more than double the old rent. I kept out from offering every person who had an indifferent character.' Stobie had achieved this considerable improvement by forming two new settlements in the area, Tighmore and Tighnacoile and redrawing the boundaries of the other settlements. By 1817 the tenants of Bohespic were described as being very poor and of indifferent character. The dyke built the previous year beside the military road had deprived them of much of the better lower ground and some of their hill pasture. Because of this, many of the farms were sublet and were being neglected. By 1826 the tenants of Easter Bohespic, Tighnacoile and Gascan were complaining that they had been deprived of their best hill pasture and left with a barren and infertile area. They maintained they were 'without the means of summering or wintering their cattle they kept to raise money for rent, their arable land being inadequate for that purpose'. A year of 'almost unprecedented drought' had left them with little food and they were unable to maintain their livestock.

The hill pasture extended to 68 soums, a soum being equivalent to a cow, or six ewes with their lambs or nine other sheep. A horse was equal to two soums. By 1855 nine soums were equivalent to each £20 of rent and the following tenants were entitled to souming:

Tenant	Original Rent			Souming Rent			Soums
	£	s	d	£	s	d	
1. Charles Robertson	16	0	0	16	0	0	7²/₁₀
2. Alex Robertson	18	0	0	18	0	0	8¹/₁₀
3. Alex McDonald	15	0	0	13	0	0	5⁸/₁₀
less £2 for 2 cottars							
4. P & John Robertson	67	0	0	53	16	0	24⁴/₁₀
less £13.4.0 for three cottars							
5. John Anderson	45	0	0	38	0	0	17¹/₁₀
deduct £7 for cottars							
6. Charles Stewart Cottar	5	14	0	5	14	0	2⁵/₁₀
7. William McGregor Cottar	6	10	0	6	10	0	2⁹/₁₀
					Total Soums		68

Souming was a method of dividing up a hill pasture occupied by several tenants and related to the number of sheep, cattle and

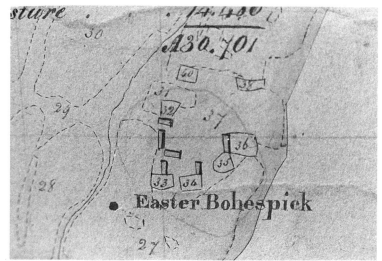

Easter Bohespic is the only one of these six settlements to have had continuous habitation, and is shown in the 1821 plan with 6 buildings.

horses suitable for a pasture. The Bohespics were sold in 1888 to Mr Tennant of Wellpark Brewery, Glasgow, for £14,000. Although this sum was acceptable, the Duke would have preferred to have sold to someone he knew, who would have been a good neighbour and kind to the tenants rather than to a complete stranger.

Wester Bohespic

The first settlement on the road to Tummelside is called *Wester or Over Bohespic* 739 610 which shows continous habitation and in 1820 contained 19 houses, with 31.4 acres of arable land, 28.8 acres of pasture and 423.5 acres of hill pasture. In 1725 Alex Robertson of Auchleeks was paying rent for the eight merk land of Wester Bohespic, which included Gascan and Dalriach, as follows:

	Scots		
	£	s	d
8 stone cheese, 8 quarts butter or 40 merks	26	13	4
Sufficient mart cow or 20 merks	13	6	8
2 Wedders and 24 poultry or	8	0	0
	£48	0	0

In 1754, there were six tenants of the 4½ merk land of Wester Bohespic, each possessing ½ merk and each paying £16 Scots in rent. The remaining 1½ merks were leased to Anne Fleeming, widow of Neil Robertson who paid £54 Scots yearly. In 1770 the tenants borrowed £24 Sterling at 7½% from the estate to build a head dyke and the interest of £1.16.0 appeared in the rentals till 1784. By 1801 the land had been divided into three equal portions, Donald Cumming taking the middle let, William Stewart the east side and William Lamont the west for a total rental of £60, well over double the £26 rental of the previous year. In 1823 the land was leased to Alex Stewart for nine years, for an annual rental of £45. Stewart was described by the factor as 'not deserving of any farm, being an encourager of vagabonds'. He also possessed a farm in Rannoch and therefore sublet the Wester Bohespic holdings to nine tenants:

Wester Bohespic Holdings 1823

Sub tenant	Rent		
	£	s	d
Duncan Stewart	4	5	0
Duncan Cumming	4	5	0
John Robertson	8	10	0
John Robertson	4	5	0
John Mcgregor	4	5	0
Duncan Robertson	8	10	0
Alex Mcgregor	4	5	0
Duncan McDonald	4	5	0
John Robertson Junior	8	10	0
Total	£51	0	0

Alex Stewart was £22.10.0 or six months in arrears with his rental payments, caused he said because his tenants were 'very bad people who never paid'. He was absent when the factor called and his wife was told that arrears in rent had to be paid or a sequestration order would be made out. A few years earlier, one of his tenants, John Robertson junior had asked to have his effects sequestrated as he had been hounded for a considerable sum. This plea arose because he was, according to the factor, 'becoming too familiar with the Athole girls who punish his pocket'.

Tighmore (great house) 741 609 lies next to Wester Bohespic and the remains of a number of dwellings can be seen, two with walls extant to 6 feet, in a wooded area. First rentals appeared in 1802 when Charles Gow was paying £25 and by 1816 this had risen to £35 when there were six houses in the settlement which consisted of 16.8 acres of arable land, 28.2 acres of pasture and 233.5 acres of hill pasture. In 1822 William Lamont obtained a three-year lease for the farm and was paying £35 a year. He was described as a 'middling good tenant' who had allowed his fences, which were once good, to fall into disrepair. His crop returns in that year were as follows:

Crop	Acres	Bolls		Price	Amount		
		Sown	Return		£	s	d
Oats	3	4	10½	15/-	7	17	6
Barley	3	3	10	17/-	8	10	0
Potatoes	1		26	6/6	8	9	0
Arable land in pasture	1		1 acre	16/-		16	0
Subset	8		8 acres		18	18	0 ˙
					£44	10	6
Pasture rent for horses and cattle on common hill					2	15	0
4 double stone wool at 7/- each					1	8	0
					£4	3	0
Keeps 80 sheep, sold 12 wedders					5	0	0
Rears 2 cattle to sell at 2 years old, This year sold for					2	5	6
					£7	5	6
Total					£55	19	0

In 1822 William Lamont was £2.18.0 in arrears with his rent and pleaded that his name should be withheld. Tighmore continued to be inhabited till the end of the 19th century, when two tenants and a cottar were paying a rental of £35 a year.

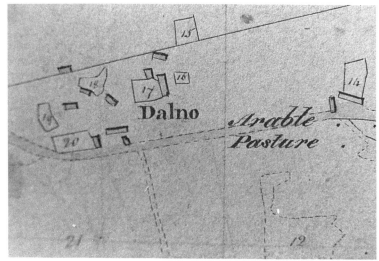

Dalno, now completely obliterated by tree planting, appears in this 1821 plan beside the military road, less than a mile from Tummel Bridge. At this time it comprised 10 buildings and various enclosures.

Gascan

Although mentioned in a 1621 charter, it was not till 1754 that *Gascan* (promontory) 745 608 became a separate unit for rentals. In that year the two merk land had five tenants paying £72 Scots amongst them. By 1820 there were three tenants paying a total of £63 Sterling and there were 18 houses in Upper Gascan and 8 in Lower Gascan, the remains of which can still be seen, with walls extant to 6 feet. In 1819 Donald and Alex Robertson, Gascan tenants, complained that their livestock were being ill-treated by their Tighnacoil neighbour James Wilson and his family, especially Mrs Wilson. Donald and Alex had lived in Gascan since 1816 and maintained that the land on the east side of the march, which had no dyke, was common pasture with their neighbour and this arrangement was established at the start. The previous summer, however, Wilson began keeping a separate and distinct march, using dogs to turn off their livestock. Since that time they 'behaved with great violence' and had injured some of their stock. Donald and Alex insisted they were entitled to use the pasture and asked the factor to intervene.

Alex Robertson, described as a 'middling good tenant', renewed his lease in 1823 and was paying £40.13.0 in rent for his farm which consisted of 17¾ acres of arable land, 21 acres of pasture and 116½ acres of hill pasture. His farm returns in that year were:

Crop	Acres	Bolls		Price	Amount		
		Sown	*Return*		£	s	d
Oats	4	5	10	15/-	7	10	0
Barley	1½	1½	5	18/-	4	10	0
Potatoes	1		20	6/6	6	10	0
Grass/hay	1						
Grass/pasture	2½		2½ acres	20/-	2	10	0
Subset	7¾		7¾ acres		18	18	0
					£39	18	0
5 stone of wool at 4/6 each					1	2	6
Pasture rent of horses and cattle on common hill					4	0	0
					£5	2	6
					£45	0	6

Rears 2 cattle to sell at 2 years old.
Sold this year for   £3   0   0
Keeps 60 sheep and lambs valued at   £3 10   0

Donald Robertson, also described as a 'middling good tenant', had his lease renewed for three years in 1823 and was paying £22.7.0 in rent. His farm comprised 10½ acres of arable, 12½ acres of pasture and 57 acres of hill pasture and his returns that year were as follows:

Crop	Acres	Bolls		Price	Amount		
		Sown	*Return*		£	s	d
Oats	5	6	9	15/-	6	15	0
Barley	2	2	8	18/-	7	4	0
Pease	½	½	1	13/-		13	0
Potatoes	1¼		40	6/6	13	0	0
Grass	1½		20st.	10d		16	8
					£28	8	8

Wool, 4 stone at 4/6 each		18	0
Pasture rent on common hill	4	0	0
		£4 18	0
		£33 6	8

He keeps 40 ewes. Has 3 lambs for sale but cannot sell them. Value perhaps		£4 16	0
Rears 2 cattle to sell at 2 years old. Sold this year worth		£5 0	0

Tighnacoil

The fourth of the Bohespic settlement is called *Tighnacoil* (house of the wood) 750 606 and there are few remains of the houses except for footings of several buildings. This was the second settlement to start in the 19th century and the 1818 rentals show that two tenants, Angus Campbell and James Wilson paid £35 between them. James Wilson was the neighbour who was the subject of the complaint by the Gascan tenants. Wilson maintained he could not obtain, 'peaceable possession' when he moved there in 1817, being subjected to 'molesting and annoyance and threats' from the people of Gascan, who had driven his wife and children off the pasture 'by stoning them nearly to death'. He therefore asked the ground officer, Alex Stewart of Woodend to establish the march between the farm and if as a result of this, the Gascan tenants decided to give up their tenancies, then he and Charles Stewart in Easter Bohespic would be ready to take over their holdings at the same rental. James Wilson contended he had always been a peaceable man and now found he had to deal with 'a band of unruly men' who thought they could achieve their own ambitions by force. Alex Stewart interviewed James Wilson and was shown a number of Gascan cattle which were trespassing on his pasture, and when herded away, were driven back again by the Gascan tenants who averred they had the right to the hill pasture as far as the Bohallie March, which was common to the farms of Tighnacoil, Gascan and Easter Bohespic.

In 1822 Duncan Stewart, described as 'rather an industrious tenant', obtained a three-year lease, at an annual rental of £26 for his farm which contained 7¾ acres of arable land, 9 acres of pasture and 135 acres of hill pasture. His farm returns were:

Crop	Acres	Bolls		Price	Amount		
		Sown	Return		£	s	d
Oats	3½	4	12	15/-	9	0	0
Barley	¾	1	3	18/-	2	14	0
Pease	½	½	1½	13/-		19	6
Potatoes	1		20	6/6	6	10	0
Grass/hay	½		30st	1/-	1	10	0
Grass/pasture	1¼		1¼ acres		1	10	0
Lint	¼	lost					
					£22	3	6

	£	s	d
4 Stone of Wool at 11/- each	2	4	0
Pasture rent for horses and cattle on common hill	5	0	0
	£7	4	0
	£29	7	6

	£	s	d
Has just 80 sheep of which he can sell 40 wedders and gimmers worth	£10	0	0

Angus Campbell, tenant since 1818, was described as a 'very bad subject' who had obtained a 15-year lease at a rental of £10 a year. His farm comprised 3¼ acres of arable land and 5½ acres of pasture and his 1822 returns were:

Crop	Bolls		Price	Amount		
	Sown	Return		£	s	d
Oats	½	1½	15/-	1	2	6
Subset to Duncan Campbell				4	15	0
				£5	17	6

Tighnacoil continued as a separate unit for rentals until it was combined with Easter Bohespic in 1858.

A late 19th century picture of Tummel Bridge and the inn, which earlier in the century was a single-storey building. It started as Wade's 'hutt' where he stayed while supervising the building of the bridge. Mendelssohn stayed here in August 1829 and in a letter home wrote of his experience: 'Evening 3 August at the Tummelbridge. The storm howls, rushes and whistles outside, slams the doors and opens the shutters. We sit quietly by the fire which I poke up at times, so that it flickers. The dining room is large and bare'.

Easter Bohespic

There has been continuous habitation of *Easter Bohespic* 755 602, sometimes known as Nether Bohespic and it is still occupied as a farm. In 1770 there were three tenants, John and Donald Robertson and Duncan Stewart, paying a rental of £5.2.3 Sterling a year and to this was added £1.1.9 being 7½% of £14 they had borrowed to build a head dyke to enclose the land. In 1803 John Campbell, a tenant, petitioned the Atholl factor because his neighbours, Peter and Alex Robertson were attempting to oust him from his farm. When the leases came up for renewal, it was the practice for one person to make improved offers for all the farms and that person's name only would appear in the rent book. Alex Robertson's son John duly made the offers for the farms which were accepted and John Campbell was then informed that John Robertson was taking over his farm as it was now in his name. 'They now stretch every nerve to dispossess me', said John Campbell who was also burdened with his father, approaching 100 years old and living with him. By 1805 John Campbell had agreed to depart and promised to remove all his furniture and cattle by Tuesday evening, 23rd July. In 1823 John Robertson paid a rental of £25 a year for his farm which contained 16¾ acres of arable land, 28¼ acres of pasture and 233¼ acres of hill pasture. He was described by the Atholl factor as being 'not a well-doing tenant, stupid and indolent'. Returns from his farm that year were:

Crop	Acres	Bolls		Price	Amount		
		Sown	Return		£	s	d
Oats	3½	4	9	15/-	6	15	0
Barley	3	3	9	17/-	7	13	0
Pease	¾	1	2	13/-	1	6	0
Turnips	1		1 acre	40/-	2	0	0
Potatoes	2		60	6/6	19	10	0
Grass/hay							
Grass/pasture	1		1 acre	20/-	1	0	0
Lint	¼	1 peck	lost				
Meadow hay			40 st	6d	1	0	0
Fallow	1						
Subset	2, plus cottages		2 acres	60/-	6	0	0
					£45	4	0

	£	s	d
10 stones wool at 7/- each	3	10	0
Pasture rent for horses and cattle on common hill	10	0	0
	£13	10	0
	£58	14	0

	£	s	d
Rears 2 cattle to sell at 2 years old	£1	10	0
Keeps 100 sheep and lambs, sold 26 wedders	£21	16	0

John Robertson was in arrears of £18.10.0 and the estate made an inventory of his farm and reported that his stock was good. This included 100 ewes and hoggs, 3 good horses, 4 cows, 4 three-year-old queys, 4 two-year-old queys plus carts, ploughs and harrows.

Dalno

Dalno (new meadows) 753 597 was located above the junction
where the military road meets the Kinloch Rannoch road and has
been completely obliterated by a forestry plantation. In 1754 it
was described as a one merk land, possessed by Duncan and
Neil Robertson who each paid £15 Scots for their half and in
1770 they commenced enclosing the land by building a head
dyke, for which they borrowed £20 at 7½% interest, followed
by a further loan of £6 in 1771 and £8 in 1772. In 1813, John
Robertson was farming the land his ancestors had worked for
the previous 150 years. He supported his wife and family and
also his six younger brothers and sisters whom he had cared
for since he was 12 years old, when his father drowned in the
River 'Tumble'. He had carried out many improvements to the
farm, including clearing stones off the fields, clearing the
woods and draining the ground at a cost of £100. Another
John Robertson, former miller at Dalcroy and described as 'the
greatest knave in that country', was subtenant of Alex Stewart
from Rannoch. His farm consisted of 7 acres of arable land, 9
acres of pasture and 100 acres of hill pasture. His neighbour
was Angus Campbell of Tighnacoil who in addition to being
described as a 'very bad subject', was known in the area as 'a
great scoundrel'. Angus paid £30 rent for his share of Dalno
and his farm returns in 1823 were as follows:

Crop	Acres	Bolls		Price	Amount		
		Sown	Return		£	s	d
Oats	4	5	10	15/-	7	10	0
Barley	2	2	3	16/-	2	8	0
Potatoes	1		30	6/6	9	15	0
Pasture	1		1 acre	40/-	2	0	0
					£21	13	0
5 stone wool					£1	10	0
					£23	3	0

He kept a tup, 30 ewes, 9 wedders, 20 hoggs and reared a stirk every year. Angus had tried to acquire the half of the land that had been cleared and drained by John Robertson, by signing for the whole area when leases were due for renewal and then claiming the land. He had no dependants having recently dispossessed, 'in the most inhuman manner', his father who had married John Robertson's widowed mother. In 1820 Angus Campbell owed £49.15.6 equivalent to 20 months' rent and within two years this had increased to £70. Although he was able to pay half in that year, he told the factor that no more money would be available for several months. By 1863 there were seven tenants paying £43.12.0 in rental and two of the ten houses were in ruins.

Tummel Bridge

The military road follows the Tummel, passes Dalno House and reaches the *Tummel Bridge* 762 592, built for Wade by John Stewart of nearby Kynachan. The contract of 25th July 1730 states that:

> 'the said John Stewart shall build a stone bridge strengthened with a double arch over the River of Tumble, which bridge is to have one arch of at least forty-two foot between the land stools. It is likewise to be twelve foot in breadth including the parapet walls, which are to be three foot high above the pavement and at least one foot broad and to be coped with good flag stones . . . and to render it easily passable for wheel carriage and cannon.'

The bridge had to be strong enough to ensure that its foundations were not damaged during 'extraordinary floods'. The price for building it was £200 Sterling, £50 to be paid on the signing of the contract and the balance on completion which John Stewart promised would be before the end of October in the same year. The builder also agreed to 'support the bridge in good repair' for 20 years, which is one of the reasons why the bridge, although by-passed by modern traffic, is still standing. The Tummel formed the boundary between the parishes of Blair Atholl and Dull and although the military road continues southwards to Aberfeldy, Crieff and beyond, this point marks the end of the road in this narrative.

CHAPTER 8

East by Tilt

Thomas Pennant travelled through the glen in 1769 and wrote a vivid account of the scene:

'Glen Tilt, famous in old times for producing the most hardy warriors, is a narrow glen, several miles in length, bounded on each side by mountains of an amazing height; on the South there is the great hill of Beinn y glo whose base is thirty five miles in circumference, and whose summit towers far above the others. The sides of many of these mountains is covered with fine verdure, and are excellent sheep-walks: but entirely woodless. The road is the most dangerous and most horrible I ever travelled: a narrow path, so rugged that our horses often were obliged to cross their legs, in order to pick a secure place for their feet; while, at a considerable and precipitous depth beneath, roared a black torrent, rolling through a bed of rock, solid in every part but where the Tilt had worn its antient way'.

When he wrote this, Pennant would have seen hundreds of people working their crofts and in their shielings, while today fewer than ten people live in the glen.

A 1350 charter confirmed to Eugene, brother of Reginald of the Isles, 'the whole Thanage of Glen Tilt, to pass for three davochs of land, in return for faithful service rendered'. For this, Eugene paid 22 merks Sterling a year and would have provided four horses for hunting once a year, if demanded. The Gaelic equivalent of Thane is Toisiche meaning leader, hence the origin of the name MacIntosh. One of their strongholds was on the east bank of the Tilt, a few hundred yards north of the Fender Burn. Called *Tom-a-Vour* 877 670, it was strongly situated on a steep bank overlooking the Tilt and was the ancient seat of the MacIntoshes of Tirinie. Barely a trace remains today, but there was a substantial ruin in the middle of the last century as Fenderbridge resident Mrs Robert Gow remembered playing in one of the doorways, when talking about it to Mr Alec MacRae in the 1930s. John, 1st Earl of Atholl acquired the Thanage from Finlay MacIntosh in 1502.

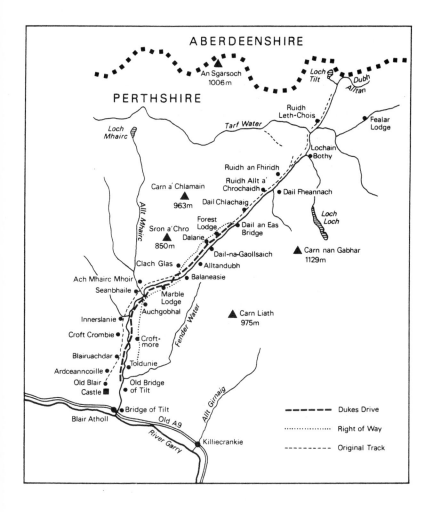

A map of Glen Tilt showing its entire length of 16 miles from the Garry confluence to the watershed at the Perthshire/Aberdeenshire boundary. Many of the 60 settlements and shielings located in the glen are marked.

This cartoon from 'Punch' shows one of the party of naturalists cocking a snook in a contemptuous gesture at two kilted ghillies as they clambered over a fence near Tibby's Lodge, in 1847 to make their escape. Their leader was Professor Balfour and his reply to an amusing ballad written about the confrontation, was:

> There's ne'er a kilted chiel
> Shall drive us back this day, man.
> It's justice and it's public richt
> We'll pass Glen Tilt afore the nicht.
> For Dukes shall we
> Care ae Bawbee?
> The road's as free
> To you and me
> As to his Grace himself, man.

At that time it consisted of 17 townships, giving an average of about a sixth part of a davoch to each. Six of those townships were located on the west side and five on the east, with a further six in Glen Fender.

The date when Alex Tarloson, alias Robertson of Lude obtained the land on the east side of Glen Tilt is uncertain. There was a time when, 'a cow may drink in the River Garry at Invertilt from which she may go on the land of the Laird of Lude without touching another man's, until she crosses the ford of Dail a Chruineachd,' where *An Lochain burn* 980 783 enters the Tilt. However, by the 18th century, Lude had lost most of his possessions in Glen Tilt, north of the Fender.

At the start there are three routes up Glen Tilt converging into two at Gow's Bridge and one beyond Forest Lodge. The route on the west side appears in Roy's Survey of 1747-1755, right through to the watershed, and serviced the settlements and shielings on that side of the glen. The 1669 Highways Act was amended around 1760, 'for making more effectual the laws for repairing the highways, bridges and ferries' and five years later the Duke of Atholl was asked to chair a committee for carrying on the new road from Blair Atholl northwards through Glen Tilt to Braemar. As early as 1758, the road from Old Blair to Allt Slanaidh, a distance of 2½ miles which included several bridges, had been much improved. The middle road is called the Drive and was completed at great expense in 1805. Lodges, gates and gate-keepers were on it and its line was lower down towards the Tilt. The Duke hoped to avoid the Right of Way and in this he was successful as apart from a short stretch north of Auchgobhal, the two routes do not coincide till beyond Forest Lodge. Queen Victoria travelled this way in 1844 and on arrival at her destination five miles up the glen, described it as an 'immense delight'. She was referring to *Marble Lodge* 898 717, at that time a keeper's cottage. She described the Tilt as, 'gushing and winding over stones and slates, and the hills and mountains skirted at the bottom with beautiful trees – the whole lit up by the sun and the air, so pure and fine, but no description can at all do it justice, or give an idea of what this drive was'.

Right of Way

The Right of Way is on the east side of the Tilt and to quote a famous court case of the last century: 'From time immemorial there has been a public road communicating between the village of Castletown of Braemar and the village of Blair Atholl'. The respondents in this case were: Mr Alexander Torrie – advocate, Mr Robert Cox – Writer to the Signet and Mr Charles Law – merchant. They maintained the road had been metalled in 1760 when it was placed under the control of the Commission of Supply of the County of Perth and had been kept in repair by statute labour. In 1853 the case was finally heard in the House of Lords and was decided against the 6th Duke. At this he evolved a plan to re-route the road out

An 1860 view of Old Bridge of Tilt. The cottage on the right was replaced by a two-storey building in the 1870s. Situated on the east bank of the Tilt, this hamlet is on the land of Lude, formed into a Barony in 1448.

of Glen Tilt but this meant passing through a few miles of Lude Estate and as Mr McInroy's demands were too steep, the matter was dropped.

The case arose originally in 1847 when a party of naturalists, six in all headed by Professor Balfour, walked through Glen Tilt. After they had proceeded for 8 or 9 miles they encountered a party consisting of two gentlemen and six attendants with dogs and guns and were ordered to return to Braemar. This they politely but firmly refused to do, stating that, as far as they knew, the road was a public one. They then passed through two locked gates and at length at the end of the glen reached another locked gate opposite Tibby's Lodge. Here a ghillie told them they could not pass without the Duke's permission. They refused to walk back to Braemar – a distance of nearly 30 miles – and apparently made their escape over a wall. Thus Messrs Torrie and others successfully brought the case against the Duke, which was the making of the Scottish Rights of Way Society.

In 1851 Old Bridge of Tilt contained 8 houses with a population of 26 including a woollen weaver, two sawmillers and a grocer. With the diversion of the main road in the 1820s,

McInroy of Lude contracted to build an inn near the new bridge over the Tilt for about £1,400 and the landlord of the old inn was offered a lease of the new one, presently known as the Tilt Hotel. The old inn was an attractive thatched cottage which was pulled down in the 1930s to make way for a sawmill.

Across the Fender, and still on the east side of the Tilt, lies the land of *Toldunie* 878 668. In 1612 William, Lord Murray, granted to Angus MacIntosh of Tirinie, the lands of Kincraigie and 'Toildowny', for a yearly feu duty of £32 Scots. The following year, it passed to Alex Robertson and in 1623 to his son Donald. In 1758, Donald Robertson of Kincraigie, who for many years had been in 'straitend' circumstances, sold the two merk land of Toldunie and forty penny land of *Croit a'Bhoineide* (croft of the bonnet) to his fourth son Charles, on condition that debts totalling 2,300 merks were paid off. Croit a'Bhoineide was named after the tenant, a bonnet-laird who paid the landlord a yearly nominal rent of a new bonnet, at the same time getting back the old one! Three years later the land was sold to James Robertson of Lude for £4,219.10.0 Scots and he promptly offered it to the 2nd Duke in exchange for the Seven Shielings in Glen Loch. This was rejected and it wasn't until 1827 that the 4th Duke purchased Toldunie and the Four Merk Land of Lude for £8,000. In the previous year the tenant, John McNaughton paid £80 rent for the parks, orchard and wood pasture with the parlour, bedroom and attic above the cottage of Toldunie. He was at liberty to plough up the arable grounds and sow oats in the first two years and barley in the third. He agreed to complete the unfinished north wing of the steading and renew the slate roof. When the land of Toldunie came up for sale in 1844 it was described as a small property containing 4½ acres of superior arable land and 25 acres of woodland. 'It has beautiful walks along the romantic scenery of both rivers and attached to it is a right of salmon fishing in the Tilt. It would form a delightful spot in the Highlands for a residence or hunting seat.' Toldunie means 'hole of the men' and tradition says that one day the ground opened up and the menfolk disappeared, to reappear across the Tilt as oxen, in a place called *Toldamh* (hole of the ox) 874 667.

The two merk land of Toldamh was one of the 17 townships

Ach Mhairc Mhoir was the largest of the Glen Tilt settlements with 27 buildings, of which many of the ruins can still be seen perched nearly 1,000 feet up the slope. The lint pool in the foreground with its inlet and outlet to the adjacent burn, was where people left their sheaves of flax to 'ret' in the running water. These pools were clay-lined and the ensuing fermentation dissolved the vegetable pith of the stalk and made it easier to separate the fibres from the woody outer stalk. The flax sheaves were then dried and transported to the lint mill.

mentioned in the Thanage of Glen Tilt in 1502. In 1601 George Leslie and his wife Margaret Stewart loaned 1,100 merks to William Murray, 2nd Earl and for this they were granted the lands of Toldamh and Walter Gald's croft for an annual rent of 4 bolls of victuals, which by 1668 had increased to 12 bolls and £16 Scots. By 1735 the land was split between two tenants, Donald Stewart and Charles Conacher, each paying £32.7.6 Scots rent, 1 poultry and 15 loads of peat and by 1758 the land had been enclosed. A year later, there were plans to build a 60 foot barn and 40 foot byre and materials included 123 joists, each 18 feet long, 8 inches broad and 4 inches thick supplied by the Atholl estate. Six masons were employed for four days, harling the inside of the barn. In 1815 the ground officer reported the discovery of two deer killed near the houses in Toldamh. He maintained that until the fence was completed between the Banvie and the Tilt, deer would continue to eat Mrs Cameron's neeps. She was the widow of James Cameron, former innkeeper in Blair and pastured 9 cows, 1 stot, 6 calves and 30 sheep on the Toldamh farmstead. The settlement was unchanged in 1830 and still occupied in the 1860s.

The road up the west bank of the Tilt, marked on Roy's Survey, starts at Old Blair and first reached *Ardceanncoille* (height of the end of the wood) 870 673, a three merk land including the ten shilling land of Bailanloan which is the present Home Farm and was not built till 1867. Ardceanncoille appears in a 1504 Charter when it was granted to William Stewart, Gentleman of the Bedchamber. In 1665 the rent was £26.13.4 and 40 loads of peat and by 1706 the settlement was providing 4 men for the Duke of Atholl's Fencibles. In his report to the 2nd Duke in 1742, Commissary Bissat the factor, commented that considering the late, bad season, tenants had paid up well and there were few arrears, excepting for this one. He said that when Robert Stewart left it 10-11 years earlier, his children had oppressed the tenants and raised the rent from £80 to £120. Since then, no one had stayed more than 2 or 3 years and were so heavily in debt that their crops were rouped to pay off arrears. 'Over the 10-11 years, four setts of broken tenants have been turned out', he wrote. In 1770 one of the tenants, George Moon, paid £3.5.0 Sterling and was bound to enclose his land at his own expense and harl his house, barn and byre with lime, and 18 years later, the land was included with Blairuachdar and struck off the rentals. It included the ten shilling land of Tynecraig, though by 1752 this was treated separately for rentals, David Stewart paying £22.2.6 Scots, which included £1 for converted peats and £1.2.6 for converted shearing.

Drumnacreich (ridge of plunder) 875 671 lay east of the road and appears in a 1601 Charter granting land to George Leslie. In 1705 it supplied six men, all of them tenants, to the Fencibles and by 1714 Robert Stewart the wadsetter was paying rent of £26.13.4 Scots, 30 loads of peat and 3 days' shearing at the Mains of Blair. By 1770 it had split into two parts, Knock and Nether Drumnacreich each with three tenants, and by 1788 the land had been included with Blairuachdar. This also happened at the same time, to *Balinuaran* (well town) 877 673, a little to the north, where nothing remains now except a few mounds in the ground, but at one time there were four tenants farming this twenty shilling land. After 1788 the land was

Marble Lodge, named after the nearby marble quarry, was built in the 1820s as a small hunting lodge. A number of untreated, quarried marble blocks lie at the roadside across from the lodge, and one of these features the initials 'J C' of the stone mason, carved into the stone. The remains of a walled enclosure, built from the houses that made up Inchgrennich, the old settlement, are behind the lodge, and the Right of Way can be seen further up the hillside.

turned over to pasture which could take 40 stots. This whole area was described by Stobie as being generally arable between the road and the Tilt and measured 203 acres.

Blairuachdar

Blairuachdar (upper plain) 874 677 was built in 1790 as the Home Farm but there were several farms here long before. In 1621 Alex McKenzie and his wife Elspeth Stewart were granted a third of the land for an annual rent of 4 bolls of victuals and 4 poultry whilst three years later Patrick Murray of Woodend acquired the 'sunny half'. This ratio changed in 1628 when Alex McKenzie obtained the 'overmost two parts' and Donald Stewart in Invervack, the 'nether third part' and the combined rent was now 60 bolls of oatmeal. By 1636, Donald Stewart had moved to Strathgroy and assigned his land to the McKenzies. The judicial rentals of 1725 show there were five tenants of this 4½ merk land. They were obliged to sow potatoes, turnips, carrots and pease, to plant 12 trees and enclose an acre or two

148

of their land each year, to thatch their houses with heather and to build a stone or clay chimney. Their shielings at this time were located up Glen Bruar.

Alex Hardy was overseer at Blairuachdar in 1796 and the factor, James Stobie, hoped he would be 'an attentive servant, diligently attending to the charge given him'. One April a few years later he was able to report that all oat sowing was completed, potato planting had started and he hoped to start barley the following week. 'Everything was going well', he concluded. In 1814 Duncan Campbell was dismissed without wages for stealing wood from a Blairuachdar plantation. He was told that if he was ever seen in any enclosure, wood or plantation belonging to the Duke, he would be dealt with according to law. Stobie in 1780 described the land of Blairuachdar as being generally arable between the road and head dyke and measuring 288 acres.

All this while, the Drive is lower down, closer to the Tilt and in Blairuachdar Wood, it crosses it at the *Cumhann-Leum Bridge* (narrow jump) 881 685, built in 1805 to complete the Drive. Our road leaves the wood at the bridge over the Croft Crombie burn. This together with the arch over *Allt an t-Seagail* (stream of the rye) 879 694, a few hundred yards up the glen, was built in 1758 at a cost of £45.0.0. This included two men working for six days, clearing the foundation for the Crombie bridge and three men for three days, preparing lime. The settlement of *Croft Crombie* (croft of the bend) 874 689 lies above the road, on an open hillside and Stobie describes this area between the road and head dyke as being generally arable and comprising 155 acres. The same applied to the area of 40 acres below the road. Croft Crombie consisted of 13 buildings, two corn-drying kilns and several enclosures. In 1621 it was granted to Neil Stewart McRobert of Urrard More and in 1773 the two tenants started to enclose the land. An item in the rentals gives us this date as the rent the previous year, of £6, had increased by 12/- representing the interest on a loan from the Duke, of £8 at 7½% for building head dykes. By 1789 Croft Crombie had been removed from the rentals and turned over to cattle grazing, along with other settlements in this part of the glen. A year later, James Stobie examined the houses and found them all in ruins. He was anxious to house a squad of labourers as

Looking down Glen Tilt from Alltandubh with the road to the marl on the left and the gable-end of the Pittenicy bothy in the middle distance. The ruins of 8 buildings are all that remain of this 25-acre farm.

close as possible to their work on the roads, and arranged for the old lint mill nearby to be fitted out for them.

Innerslanie 879 696 was of a comparable size, containing 14 buildings and 2 kilns and became depopulated in 1789. It was often linked with Ach Mhairc Mhoir further up the glen, and these lands were granted to Malcolm Stewart, second son of John Stewart of Shierglas in 1637. In 1669 Alex Stewart was empowered to employ Alex Frangach to kill 20 deer for the 2nd Earl. He was to be paid 20/- Scots for each hart and a merk for each hind and as he had been appointed forester within the bounds of Tarf and Beinn a' Ghlo, was permitted to kill two deer for himself and any lame ones he found. Enclosing started in 1772 when £3 was loaned at 7½% for building head dykes and £33 was advanced the following year, the additional £2.14.0 interest continuing to be paid right up to 1784.

After crossing the *Allt Slanaidh* (healing stream) bridge, built when this part of the road was completed in 1759, we pass a level piece of ground of an acre or two and this is where the glen folk grew their potatoes. That brings us to *Gilbert's Bridge* 881 701 formerly known as the Balvenie Bridge, built in

1759. It was named after a hillman called William Gilbert Robertson who lived in the nearby cottage, later to be occupied by Elly Campbell renowned for spreading butter with her thumb! It was a lean-to with plastered walls featuring a striking set of drawings until it was demolished in the 1950s.

Our road turns off to the left just before the bridge and here until recently, it was a well-made walker's track, cut into the hillside. In a few hundred yards we reach *Ach Mhairc Bhig* (little field of the horse) 882 705 – 100 years ago in a cleared area of ground – now completely overgrown with trees, but enough remains to indicate that at one time there were three or four buildings and a kiln here. Stobie describes this as 34 acres of arable land. This was a twenty shilling (1½ merk) land and was given to John Stewart, eldest son of Neil Stewart of Shierglas in 1618. In 1665 its rent was £40 Scots plus casualties which consisted of a lamb, a kid, a wedder, 12 poultry, 60 loads of peat from the hill above, and a day's shearing at the Mains of Blair. Malcolm Stewart, the wadsetter, was involved in the 1715 uprising, his lands forfeited and he was deported from Preston in 1726. In 1772 the rent was £4.4.0 Sterling as well as two carriages of three horses from Dunkeld to Blair, two carriages from Rannoch or Mar and three deer. The tenant was also responsible for building 100 roods of dyke at his own cost. Half a merk of this twenty shilling land was called *Seanbhaile* (old town) 888 711, a 23½ acre settlement. Here, footings of several buildings can be seen on level ground, 100 feet above the Tilt, while further up the hillside are substantial remains of nine buildings with walls 3 feet-4 feet high. Alex Crerar took a 19-year lease in 1770 at a rent of £3.3.0 and contracted to enclose the land within six years.

Ach Mhairc Mhoir

As the track climbs away from the Tilt, it crosses Allt Mhairc by the Ach Mhairc Mhoir bridge, a sturdy single arch across a cataract, to reach a settlement of the same name. *Ach Mhairc Mhoir* (big field of the horse) 888 715 consisted of 27 buildings, four kilns and several enclosures, within an area of lazy-bed cultivation and clearance heaps. The remains vary from grass-covered footings to substantial dry-stone walls, some standing to gable height, suggesting two phases of depopulation.

Forest Lodge seen from high up the hillside across the Tilt. It was built in 1779 and considerably enlarged in the 19th century. The early building was described by William Scrope, the sportsman, as consisting of 'two tenements united by a stone screen surmounted by stags' horns and in which there is an archway for carriages to pass. One of these tenements was for the Lord of the Forest and his friends and the other for his retinue'.

Adjacent to one of these there is a lint pool where the inlet from a nearby stream and out-flow can still be seen. One of the buildings features a drain and was used as a cattle byre. The settlement falls into two distinct parts, many of the buildings being situated lower down, on level ground close to the bridge, with the remainder further up the hill on open land. Ach Mhairc Mhoir appears in a Charter of Sale by Andrew, Thane of Glen Tilt to Neil Stewart of Fothergill in 1461, and in 1668 the rent was £26.13.4 Scots with 100 loads of peat. In 1707 the wadsetter Alex Stewart was told to collect as many Fencible men as possible from the parish and take them with their arms to guard the Duke's holding at 'Killmavennark'. Here, he was to ensure that good order was maintained and anyone guilty of drunkenness, swearing or causing a riot would be held until they could be dealt with by the law. Before linking up with the Drive, our road passes near one more settlement, *Tighnacoil* (house of the wood) 901 720. This is situated on a steep slope

152

of Sron a' Chro and consisted of five buildings and a kiln, immediately above Gow's Bridge.

Right of Way

Now, we must retrace our steps to pick up the Right of Way on the east side of Glen Tilt, where it leaves the road below the farm of Kincraigie. *Creag Mhic an Toisiche* (MacIntosh's rock) 881 690 lies in the river, far below. It was here that the Thane sat when he held his Court once a year and apparently a man was executed on each occasion. Mercifully, the Court took place only when he could reach it dryshod, hence the Gaelic saying: 'It is not every day that MacIntosh holds his Court'.

The first settlement, at a height of over 1,000 feet is called *Ard Campsie* (point of the bent stance) 887 687. The area included Nether Campsie and Croftmore and according to Stobie in 1780 was generally arable to the extent of 119 acres and rent was often taken collectively. The Campsies, along with Croftmore, Dalginross and Little Lude in Glen Fender, were purchased by Alexander Robertson of Lude, in 1607. In 1793 there were three tenants in Ard Campsie each with a third of the land and paying a rent of £8.12.1. Likewise in Nether Campsie there were two tenants paying £7 between them. In 1801 they offered £10 and £8 respectively, but this was rejected and both Campsies were in ruins by 1808. The whole area was leased to John Robertson, who by 1814 was paying £105 for the sheep pasture. It was he who in the same year sought permission to rebuild and thatch the houses in Ard Campsie and construct a cart shed measuring 70 feet by 20 feet to be built between the south gable of the byre and sit-house. 'If they are built with mortar and seethed with lime, I will pay the percentage', he said. 'The Croftmore doors would fit the houses in Upper Campsie'. Permission was refused. There is no trace of Nether Campsie though it was located near Allt na Ba and it has completely disappeared with the planting of the Leathad Mor wood. By 1680 Croftmore had reverted back to the Atholl estate and in that year, John, 1st Marquis, granted the land to Donald Stewart of Pitnacree and his wife Marjorie Robertson who by1707 were paying an annual rent of £30 Scots, a wedder and 30 loads of peat from the moss at Moine Mhor. The *Croftmore farm* (big croft) 882 687 was built in 1809

A shooting party seen leaving Forest Lodge around the turn of the century, with up to eight men employed in the shoot. There was the stalker with his telescope, a man to carry the rifle, a ponyman with pony to carry the dead deer back to the lodge, a man to 'gralloch' the deer and another to control the dogs.

and the tenancy now shared with John Stewart in Strathgroy, described as one of the best farmers in Atholl. By this time the whole area was under sheep, tenants having left when their leases ran out thus leaving the way clear for all arable ground to be put under grass.

John Robertson was again seeking assistance by requesting glass to mend the broken windows of Croftmore and also timber for beds and closets which he had been promised sometime earlier. He also maintained that several of the slates were broken. However by 1816 he was in trouble with his rent and his effects in Croftmore were rouped to pay off his arrears. He listed a number of complaints against the factor, one of them being that he was charged for wintering his beasts on another part of the plantation on the promise that it would not be overstocked. Within a month they were 'reduced to perfect skeletons' and though seven of the 33 had died, his plea for exemption of payment was rejected. By then the area was over-run with sheep and the overseer felt that the numbers should be reduced to keep them off the Croftmore planting.

There was not enough grass to feed so many and by night they were coming down to eat the crops.

Auchgobhal

A further mile brings us to *Auchgobhal* (field of the fork) 885 706, in 1780 an arable farm of some 42 acres. On 25th May 1590 a contract was drawn up by William Murray, 2nd Earl of Tullibardine granting this land to Beatrix Leslie, spouse to John Stewart, with the privilege of leading and winning peats from the hill above Ach Mhairc Bhig. In 1729 there were five tenants here, paying amongst them £144 Scots and a loan for building dykes of £4 Sterling was made in 1771. This was followed by £5 in 1772 and a further £1 the next year – the interest of 15/- being added to the rental. By 1808 the settlement contained at least eight buildings and in 1820 the tenant was Robert Stewart who had over eight acres for crops. 4½ acres were sown with oats, with a return of just over twofold, barley produced a threefold return, and he also planted pease, potatoes and ¼ acre for lint. This would have been retted in the two lint pools a few hundred yards up the road. He also provided winter pasture for 35 sheep, but was heavily in debt, to the tune of £50 – a year's rent.

In 1776 the Scottish Society for the Propagation of Christian Knowledge opened a charity school here under the charge of Duncan Ferguson. He was paid £10 a year to teach 40 boys and 13 girls. By 1781 he had 56 pupils but on 6th May 1788, the school was closed and Ferguson moved to Orchilmore, near Aldclune. In 1831 the farm was let for grazing to James MacDonald for £76 a year, but he had other ideas and eventually relinquished his lease. Shortly after this, the two locked gates, which were featured in the Right of Way case were erected, one on each side of the farm. At this point the Right of Way passes at the back of the farm and here it is very clear as it descends to the Drive. By 1860 Auchgobhal was in ruins, but was rebuilt for Peter Fraser, ex-head forester, who had moved from Forest Lodge to make room for the shooting tenant.

The *Queen's Well* 890 710 is on the right of the road and opposite the confluence of Allt Mhairc and the Tilt. It was here during Queen Victoria's stay in the castle in 1844, that a groom was sent each morning to fill a bottle at the small spring of fine pure water issuing from a rock. A little further on there is *Leum nam Brog* (leap of the boot) 890 713. John Stewart, alias Black Jock, lost a shoe when leaping across the river to win a wager and that brings us to *Inchgrennich* (gathering meadow) 898 717, an arable farm of 12 acres in 1780. Initially it came under the Fas Charaidh tenant but in 1786 it was divided two thirds with Auchgobhal and the remaining third with Pittenicy and by 1808, was in ruins. By the 1820s it was called Marble Lodge after the recently-opened marble quarry, when a small shooting lodge was built there and in 1827 a shed was built to serve as a coach and peat house thus freeing one of the apartments for use as a stable.

Gow's Bridge

The Right of Way passes behind Marble Lodge and follows a line a few yards higher up than the Drive, which crosses the Tilt at this point by means of *Gow's Bridge* 901 717 also completed in 1759. Initially it was called Stewart's Bridge but in the time of the 4th Duke, became known as Gow's Bridge after a man who allegedly kept a public house nearby. It and Gilbert's Bridge were built by John MacDonald, mason from Dunkeld. His price was:

	£	s	d
Two 50ft. arch bridges	105	0	0
Timber	43	10	9
Carpenters, garden men, carts, horses	20	0	0
Lime at 9d boll.			
430 bolls for Gilbert's bridge	16	2	6
506 bolls for Gow's bridge	18	19	6
Wrights' wages. John McLarran 45 days at 1/6 day	3	7	6
William Wallace, John Wallace. 11 days at 1/- day	1	2	0
Grand total for the two bridges	£208	2	3

Marble Quarry

The marble quarry 903 718 is on the east bank of the Tilt and the track down to it, completed in 1815, leaves the Drive just before Gow's Bridge. The presence of a marble seam was first brought to the Duke's notice by the Scottish Geological Society in 1813 and by the following year, marble blocks had been dispatched to Dundee for shipment to London. Scrope describes the quarry as containing 'immense blocks of marble, varying from grass green to ones of a yellower cast intermixed with grey. The best blocks take a good polish. There is also a beautiful yellow marble mottled with white, as well as a coarse sort of white marble polluted with grey streaks'. Occasionally, a block of blue marble was quarried. Green was the most popular marble produced while the white, being coarser, had a tendency to fracture and by 1830, production of this colour had ceased. The yellow marble proved extremely difficult to cut and was rarely quarried.

Up to eight men worked the quarry and their wages ranged from 1/4d a day up to 2/- for the foreman and monthly wages in 1820 totalled £13.1.8. Weekly output averaged four blocks, measuring from 8½ feet to 3 feet in length, depending on demand and in a three month period, 12 blocks of white and 36 of green were quarried. Three of the men were employed in turning the blocks, while the rest were boring and quarrying. Sometimes the stone mason would cut his initials on to the block and there is an example opposite Marble Lodge with the initials 'J.C.'. The blocks would then be assembled, boxed and carted to Inver near Dunkeld, where there was a marble sawmill and grinding and polishing mill. The polishing mill had an improved plan for moving the table sideways, and the cost for building and equipping it was £90.11.2. The sawmill featured a new machine for sawing marble with improvements to enable the saw to cut flat surfaces and cost £112.15.0.

In 1816 marble blocks started to be sent to Edinburgh and the price charged was a guinea per cubic foot. In Messrs. Burns & Co. yard there were two blocks, one 7 feet in length – 11.3 cubic feet, the other 4 feet 9 inches in length – 6 cubic feet, totalling 17.3 cubic feet in stock, price £18.4.0. By 1821 the Duke had appointed an agent, William Reid of Edinburgh who was granted marble at 13/4d per cubic foot and planned to make chimney-pieces and table tops, but almost immediately he ran into quality problems Reid claimed that in the depot at Dunkeld, there were 50 bocks for sale, two thirds of which were useless and the remainder being of such poor quality, would cost twice as much to prepare. He already had six

The old bridge called Dail an Eas, half-a-mile beyond Forest Lodge. This graceful stone arch across the Tilt fell down a few years ago and was not replaced.

chimney pieces in stock, one 'very massive' which would sell for £26 and he asked the Duke to recommend them to possible customers e.g. the National Monument to be erected in Edinburgh, and for the alterations proposed at Perth County Hall because he thought the Duke might be able to 'exert influences in those quarters'. By 1830 due to foreign imports, the price had dropped to 6/- per cubic foot and the quarry was becoming uneconomic, though it was still producing at the end of the decade, as £5.9.1 was spent in 1839 for repairing tools. The Right of Way continues to follow the east bank, climbs above the marble quarry and crosses the Tilt by means of a ford between Dail Mhoraisd and Pittenicy. There were plans in 1759 to build a single arch bridge here for 50 guineas, but the idea was not pursued.

Marl

High above the track is the Pittenicy Marl, where it oozes from the hillside. Plans to exploit marl were drawn up in 1812 and the franchise given to John Robertson, miller of Quiech. One of the conditions was that the road would be built by the tenants thus reducing the cost to John Robertson and because of this he had no hesitation in signing the agreement, believing it would be 'a great stimulus to vegetation'. But the road was not completed till the following year and at great expense to himself and he then discovered that tenants were not prepared to try the marl till they could see the results. So he sent his man to 'dig and pick it out among the stones' and transport a few loads to Croftmore so that he could demonstrate its benefits. By 1815 the road was described as 'good', plenty of marl was available, Strathgroy farm had already taken 60 bolls and other tenants were becoming interested. His account for that year showed 115 bolls at 1/- boll and 40 bolls at 1/3d, totalling £8.5.0.

Pittenicy (portion of the stance) 910 719, an 8-acre farm in 1780, contains the remains of eight buildings and enclosures around a bothy, still used in the summer months. In 1657 Duncan Stewart and his wife Janet Robertson were granted these fifteen shilling lands, divided into 'sunny' and 'shadow' halves and in 1665 the rent was £6.13.4 Scots plus a kid, a lamb, 12 poultry, 50 loads of peat and a day's shearing at the Mains of Blair. In 1705 the settlement was providing seven men for the Fencibles. According to the ground officer, it was very fertile – 'not another spot that yields so much', he said. Despite this, in 1802 the leases ran out, along with Alltandubh and Dail-na-Gaollsaich further up the glen and the three were added to the Duke's sheep pasture in that year and sown with clover. By the middle of the last century, the name had been changed to Balaneasie.

Alltandubh (little black stream) 915 723, next up the glen, was another fertile farm of 25 acres where remains of eight buildings, one of them substantial, with enclosures and a kiln, are visible. In 1729 this was a shieling possessed by John Stewart of Dail Mhoraisd but within 25 years, it had become a permanent settlement with a rental of £50 Scots, which by 1802, the last year of tenancy, had increased to £10 Sterling. Next we come to the shieling of *Ruigh Dorcha* (dark shieling) 922 730 which is located on both sides of the burn of the same name. It was part of the next settlement, *Dail-na-Gaollsaich* 925 734, a farm of almost 20 acres where the remains of eight buildings can be seen, with two detached from the main settlement, along with a kiln. When Dail Chlachaig was cleared

Three of the magnificent corries that form part of the Beinn a' Ghlo mountain range. The track up the glen passes below them and it is easy to understand that a shot fired in one corrie cannot be heard by someone in the next one.

in 1783, John Robertson the tenant was settled here with a rental of £2.13.9 and he remained till 1802 when the area was turned over to sheep. *Dail Mhoraisd* (haugh of great growth) 909 720 lies across the Tilt from Balaneasie and at one time contained 16 dwellings, an open-ended byre and a specially built-up area of fertile ground. A flood embankment had been built where *Allt Craoinidh* (stream of the gatherer) bends as it enters the Tilt and some of the houses butted onto the banking. It was severe flooding which caused the demise of this settlement. A 1637 Charter granted these lands to John MacIntosh and Janet Rattray when the rental was £30.10.0 Scots. By 1785 the land was leased along with three settlements further up the glen, to Ralph Hall, the Duke's principal servant or household steward for £25 Sterling. One of the conditions was that he should build a march dyke at his own expense, between his farm and Tighnacoil. Precise specifications were drawn up for building these dykes. Normally the height was 5 feet 3 inches, including a 9 inch high coping of large flattish stones set on edge and projecting an inch or two each side with foundations 34 inches wide tapering to 14 inches at the top.

The cost was 6/- to 7/- per six Scottish ells though this would vary, not so much because of scarcity of stones but with the ease with which they could be broken up. The length of dyke to be built in a day would be decided by the mason throwing his hammer, the point where it landed being the distance. Therefore the fitter he was, the further the hammer was thrown! This particular dyke climbs to the top of Sron a' Chro, a height of over 2,500 feet where it joins another dyke built by the Duke in 1786/87, which crosses the hills north of the glen, enclosing the Forest of Tarf.

Immediately after the bridge at Dail Mhoraisd, the Right of Way branches to the left, to hug the hillside, while the Drive runs across a flat piece of ground nearer the river. It was here in *Clachglas* (grey stone) 916 726 that Ralph Hall was obliged to maintain a steading which later was improved as a headman's house. It was let to the Duke of Buccleuch in 1834 as a shooting hut. Climbing steeply up the hillside behind, there is a peat road connecting with the moss right up Allt Craoinidh. In 1780 Clachglas was a mainly arable farm of 26 acres, and the remains of four buildings and a kiln can be seen beside the Right of Way. Opposite, crossing the Tilt is *Drochaid na Roinnag* (bridge of the wisp of wool) – a flimsy wooden bridge. It is perched high up on two stools of rock, high enough to escape the worst ravages of the Tilt in spate, though there are times when it is completely isolated by the volume of water.

Craig Dhearg (red crag) 923 736 was a 9-acre farm beside the Right of Way and at one time contained eight buildings and a kiln, though the remains are barely visible. In 1679 William MacIntosh, the tenant, was paid half a boll of meal, 1 stone of cheese, 1 lb of powder and 4½ lb of lead shot for assisting the stalker to kill deer that year. By 1742 this settlement had become a merk land, divided between two tenants who each paid £36.6.8 Scots and 15 loads of peat and by 1784 it had been leased to Ralph Hall. *Poll Te* (woman's pool) is in a bend of the river. Living nearby in Dail-na-Gaollsaich was a couple from Glen Fender, where the man was so obnoxious that the poor wife committed suicide by throwing herself into the pool. The Right of Way stays close to the hillside and passes behind *Dalarie* (special haugh) 929 738, an arable farm of 13 acres in 1780. This was part of Craig Dhearg so there are no rental details until Ralph Hall was granted the land for sheep. Stables were built in 1811. The Right of Way branches off to the left of the Drive and rejoins it after half a mile, passing round the back of Forest Lodge.

Forest Lodge

Forest Lodge 933 741 does not appear on Stobie's 1780 map, although it was built the year before. This was described as a shooting lodge with two rooms and was considerably enlarged in the 19th century. It was built near a place called *Dalness* (haugh of the waterfall) 936 745 located a few hundred yards north of the lodge, where the remains of two buildings and an enclosure are visible. When Ralph Hall's lease ran out, Dalness was taken over by the Duke, a dyke built to form a park and a barn also erected. Near it was the Dail an Eas Bridge a little to the north. In 1796 the Hon. Sarah Murray described it thus: 'About a quarter of a mile above the lodge is a small simple bridge, of one arch, over the Tilt, and a fall of the river under it, very pretty indeed.' This beautifully-proportioned bridge fell down a few years ago and has not been rebuilt.

At this point, the glen starts to narrow again and on the west bank, almost hidden in the trees, is *Dail Chlachaig* (haugh of the little stones) 947 754. According to Stobie this was an arable farm of nearly 10 acres and was enclosed in 1772 when the rent increased by 3/9d to £2.13.9, the increase being 7½% of £2.10.0 advanced for building a dyke. This settlement was closely linked with *Chlachag* (place of little stones) 954 760 which was a larger arable farm of some 23 acres. Across the water stands the shieling of *Dail Allt na Caillich* (haugh of the stream of the old woman) 956 761 where the remains of a few bothies are visible on level ground. This shieling was claimed as the most northerly point of the Tilt/Fender Commonty boundary by Patrick Robertson in 1656. This matter was always a bone of contention between Atholl and Lude and no agreement was ever found. It was part of the larger shieling of *Dail Fheannach* (shaggy haugh) 959 762, which became an arable farm of over 20 acres, where scattered on both sides of the Tilt are the remains of 16 dwellings and several enclosures. A 1590 contract gave to Beatrix Leslie, 'Achgowill with the shieling of Dal Fheannach' and this arrangement remained till

1735, when it was taken over for a sheep pasture. Four years later, the Duke's herd there, Patrick Murray, requested payment of 2 pecks of meal a month for killing 13 deer the previous year. In 1740 he received £6 Scots for killing deer for the Duke's use.

The shieling of *Ruidh Allt a' Chrochaidh* (shieling of the hanging stream) 957 764 is west of the Tilt, opposite a wooden footbridge rebuilt and heightened in 1902. This shieling had five buildings, one of them round, and was leased to Dail Mhoraisd tenants in 1669. By 1687 they were paying a stone of cheese, a quart of butter and a wedder (total conversion rate £25.6.0 Scots) for this shieling and Allt-na-Maraig, further down. The glen gets even narrower at this point, yet on shelves high up the hillsides there are a number of shielings. *Ruidh an Fhirich* (shieling of high ground) 966 777 south of Allt Mhean contained at least 40 circular, oval or rectangular shieling bothies and an enclosure. In a 17th century charter it was leased to tenants of Dalginross, the Campsies and Croftmore.

When Pennant was travelling this way in 1769, he would have taken a track called the Dunmore Walk close to this shieling, to cross the Tarf by a ford called *Athan Feith Mharcaidh* (ford of the stream of horses' place) 957 797, thereby avoiding the dangerous crossing at the Falls. He gives us a vivid description of a shieling which could easily have been this one:

'Ascend a steep hill and find ourselves on an Arrie, or tract of mountain which the families of one or two hamlets retire to with their flocks for pasture in summer. Here we refreshed ourselves with some goat's whey at a sheelin, or Bothay, a cottage made of turf, the dairy-house, where the Highland shepherds, or graziers, live with their herds and flocks, and during the fine season make butter and cheese. Their whole furniture consists of a few horn-spoons, their milking utensils, a couch formed of sods to lie on, and a rug to cover them. Their food oat-cakes, butter or cheese, and often the coagulated blood of their cattle spread on their bannocks. They drink milk, whey, and sometimes, by way of indulgence, whiskey.'

This shieling is opposite three of the 28 magnificent Beinn a' Ghlo corries. 'These corries, though contiguous, are separated from each other by such high ridges that a person standing in one of them could not hear a shot fired in the next', noted

The confluence of the An Lochain Burn and the Tilt beside the ford at Dail a' Chruineachd, 12 miles from Blair Castle. This was the furthest point up the glen belonging to the Barony of Lude on the east side, and also the location of a sumptuous royal feast which took place in 1529.

William Scrope at the beginning of the last century.

Another shieling on this shelf is *Ruidh Allt Mheann* (shieling of the stream of the kids) 973 778 where the remains of six bothies can be seen. Tenants came from Ach Mhairc Mhoir, and Innerslanie on the west side of the Tilt and paid a rental of 3 wedders or £6 Scots a year in 1687. Further up the hillside, there is *Ruidh Feith an Duin* (shieling of the stream of the hill fort) 970 786 where there are the remains of seven buildings, some with walls 4 feet high and two with small circular annexes. Again it was tenants from lower down the Tilt, in Dalginross and the Campsies who pastured their livestock here. Another shieling on this shelf is called *Ruidh an Duin* (shieling of the hill fort) 975 781 where there were twelve oval or rectangular bothies, three of them substantial, with two small enclosures and two detached store houses. This was leased to the bowmen of Craig Dhearg in 1669. Below here, An Lochain joins the Tilt, coming from Loch Loch. This is where the ford of Dail a' Chruineachd is located – mentioned in that early Lude charter as being the furthest point up the glen that

164

his cow could drink water from the Tilt without straying off his land. In front of the ford are the remains of Bothan Dail a' Chruineachd. This was built over a three-week period in 1792 by eight men and was thatched with heather, John Stewart and James Stewart, masons, being paid 1/8d a day and the rest 1/- a day. At about 3 p.m. on 9th October 1861, Queen Victoria lunched here during her journey to Balmoral land she described the scene as 'looking up a glen towards Loch Loch, on a high bank overhanging the Tilt. Looking back, the view was very fine'.

Royal Feast

The area of level ground on the east side was the site of a gigantic hunt which was held in the Atholl mountains in 1529. It was here that the Earl of Atholl had built a temporary palace to accommodate and entertain his distinguished guests – King James V, accompanied by his mother Queen Margaret and the Pope's ambassador. The palace was made from green timber, the floors laid with turf, reeds and flowers, decorated with fine tapestries and silk drapes and 'lighted with fine glass windows in all pairts'. A three-storey block house stood at each corner, and the way in was over a drawbridge, across a pool, 16 feet deep and 30 feet broad, stocked with salmon, trout, perch, pike and eels, and finally, entrance was gained through a portcullis. The entertainment was equally lavish. A variety of red and white wine and beer was provided with beef, mutton, lamb, veal, venison, goose, partridge, plover, duck, swan and many others. The King stayed for three days and the ambassador was amazed to find such a sumptuous palace and such excellent fare in so remote a place. But he was dumbfounded when he saw the highlanders set fire to the palace as soon as the hunting had finished. 'Such is the practice of our Highlanders that however well they might have lodged for the night, they always burn their lodgings before they leave' said King James. Vestiges of the palace could still be seen at the end of the 18th century.

The *Lochain Bothy* 982 781 is located a few hundred yards up the burn. It was built over 120 years ago and subsequently burnt down. This was where the 6th Duke planned to divert the Right of Way from the lower part of the glen. His plan was to replace the ford with a bridge and build a new road up the Lochain Burn, along the east side of Loch Loch. It would have joined the Shinagag Road to finish at Old Bridge of Tilt. Much of the time the road would have passed through the Seven Shielings, land owned by the Duke, but on which Lude had the grazing rights. Four to five miles of new road would be constructed and as the route would have crossed McInroy of Lude's land the Duke offered to pay compensation. Although for only a mile or two, Lude would only have considered it if the Duke were to offer exclusive shooting rights in perpetuity over the Seven Shielings, and this was out of the question. 'This proposal is offensive in its character. The proposed transference of an obnoxious burden involves a proposal of somewhat ungracious character,' claimed Lude. 'Droves of cattle and passengers along the public road would constantly disturb my cattle and sheep.'

The shieling of *Ruidh na Cuile* (shieling of the nook) 985 784 lies on the north side of the Lochain Burn and covers a large area of pasture land. Glen Tilt tenants from Ach Mhairc Bhig and Chlachag used this pasture during the summer months, the earliest reference being in 1656.

Falls of Tarf

From here it is a short step to the Falls of Tarf and the *Bedford Bridge* 983 796. It was on 25th August 1879 that two English tourists tried to cross the swollen river. One succeeded, but the other, Francis John Bedford, an 18-year-old student, was swept away and this bridge was built in 1886 to commemorate his death. Crossing at this point was always dangerous and sometimes in the middle of the ford, the water could be waist high, Queen Victoria describing it as 'the celebrated ford of Tarff'. The glen folk, returning from Braemar with their meal, sometimes lost part of it here. The timber they used for making furniture came on horseback from Braemar and getting it across this ford must have presented problems. In 1822 Fealar Lodge to the east was burgled, 18 bottles of claret drunk, porter, hams and other things eaten or removed and the robbers, in attempting to cross the Tarf, lost a horse as the water was so high at the ford. A single-arch stone bridge was built here in 1770 by John Stewart, mason, at a cost of £29.4.0.

of which £6 was for 120 bolls of lime at 1/- a boll. This was taken down at the start of the Right of Way dispute in 1819 in an effort to deter tourists.

The shieling of *Ruidh Leth-Chois* 984 800, alias Rienacallich, is located above the junction of the two feeder rivers where the River Tilt begins, and where the old road to Fealar starts. Here, the remains of five oval shielings are visible along with a number of rectangular buildings. Ruidh Leth-Chois means shieling of one foot and it was here that Comyn's horse was found, foaming at the mouth, and all that remained of Walter's body was a leg hanging out of the stirrup. Prior to 1669 it was possessed by the bowmen in Campsie, but in that year the Earl's bowmen in Craig Dhearg became tenants. In 1704 the tenant, Alex Stewart of Innerslanie was cited in a forest-abuse paper as having a shieling which was the most damaging to the forest, being the very place where the hinds were accustomed to calve. An informant indicated that before the shieling was built he had seen over 1,000 hinds there but now there were not even 50. Also he was accused of pasturing beasts from neighbouring glens and of collaborating with the Badenoch foresters who were killing deer within the Duke's forests. By 1720, there were three tenants here: Alex Stewart of Innerslanie, Aeneas MacPherson from Killihuntly in Glen Tromie and his forester John McIntosh. Aeneas MacPherson's agreement of that year gave him a shieling called Rienacallich but only in the summertime. The shieling called *Ruid an t-Sluichd* (shieling of the pit) 986 799 lies at the foot of Ruidh Leth-chois and was leased to Thomas Stewart, forester in 1720. It is on level ground at the junction of the two rivers and consisted of three buildings, close to the ford pointing to the old route to Fealar, which climbs steeply up the ridge of Tulach Breac. South of the river is the large shieling of *Ruidh Niall* (Neil's shieling) 989 797 where there is a vast expanse of grassland on the hilltops. Ruidh Niall was given to John McPhaul from Auchgobhal in 1687 in lieu of Dail Fheannach and he paid no money, but casualties of a stone of cheese, a quart of butter and a wedder. The way to this shieling is from the Glen Tilt direction, by means of a path which zigzags up the hillside.

The path continues along the west side of *Allt Garbh Buidhe*

This old print shows Queen Victoria crossing the River Tarf below the Falls in 1861 on her way back to Balmoral. Remains of the buttress of the old stone bridge demolished in 1819 are visible on the right. Members of the party included (right to left): Charles Stewart followed by two pipers of the Atholl Highlanders; the 6th Duke leading the Queen's pony, with John Brown to her right and Sandy McAra, head keeper on her left; the Prince Consort closely followed by Princess Alice in front of her fiancé Prince Louis of Hesse.

(rough yellow stream) and here the glen is at its narrowest. Queen Victoria described the road at this point as becoming 'almost precipitous, and, indeed, very unpleasant to ride but being wet, and difficult to walk, we ladies rode. . . We emerged from the pass upon an open valley'. Here is the shieling called *Ruidh Caochan Dubh* (shieling of the black stream) 996 820 which contains the substantial remains of five dwellings and two store-houses. Aeneas MacPherson was granted the lease of this shieling in 1718: 'To sheall on the haugh at the foot of the burn coming out of Loch Tilt, near the march of our forest with the forest of Marr, for payment of one stone of butter'. Loch Tilt lies above the shieling and it was here that Pennant, on his journey to Braemar, stopped for lunch. 'Dined on the side of Loch-Tilt, a small piece of water, swarming with Trouts,' he wrote.

Finally, we reach the watershed marked by *Dubh Alltan* (little black stream) 001 825 which flows close to the march. Apparently the men of Braemar once attempted to dig a trench through the level part in order to divert this burn so that it would flow into the Dee rather than the Tilt. They were routed by the Atholl men and the course of Dubh Alltan remained uncharged.

Decline

Many of the Glen Tilt settlements were sited at over 1,000 feet and some nearly 1,500 feet and by the 18th century, the problem of existence in these upland glens was intensifying. The value of the soil was decreasing as internal movement increased and with a growing population and more livestock, severe degeneration of already poor land took place. The oats and barley returns achieved in Auchgobhal in the 1820s indicate this. There were immense difficulties in working the arable ground because of the steepness of the slope, the smallness and scattered nature of the holdings, many of which could not be amalgamated because of the terrain. Sometimes it was the sheer inaccessibility of the farmsteads, which was their downfall. Life became one of bare subsistence and to quote from the Blair Minister the Rev. John Stewart, writing of the glen in 1838: 'In former times, the higher grounds were inhabited by numerous tenants. Their possessions were small; their supply of farinaceous foods was precarious, and in the very best seasons, afforded but a scanty subsistence. They had no potatoes, and their principal aliment was animal food.'

The change of emphasis in the middle of the 18th century from services to cash for rentals forced landlords, because of an ever-widening economic environment, to create new conditions by introducing sheep, which in their turn brought their own problems. Cattle at best were more general grazers, keeping down the coarser grass, but sheep ate everything. In this new situation therefore, the small crofter could not exist. In 1785 the leases of four tenancies on the west side – Dail Mhoraisd, Clachglas, Craig Dhearg and Dalarie ran out and were not retaken by their former tenants. They were therefore granted to Ralph Hall who turned the whole area into a large sheep run. Four years later, Ach Mhairc Bhig, Ach Mhairc Mhoir which included Seanbhaile, and Tighnacoil leases ran out and were turned over to sheep. On the east side, some further rationalisation and amalgamation occurred. Inchgrennich became part of Auchgobhal in 1785 and the advent of the marble quarry changed its character in 1815. The Campsies were absorbed by Croftmore in 1802 and the leases of Pittenicy, Alltandubh and Dail-na-Gaollsaich terminated in the same year largely through their inaccessibility – the road was on the other side of the Tilt.

We have already seen examples where the Atholl estate arranged to resettle a tenant when his lease expired. Another happened in 1784 when those tenants who had lost their shielings at the head of the Glen were given the shieling of Allt na Saobhaidh in the Glaschorie near Glen Bruar as recompense, and there are several more examples of a similar nature. In 1909 a committee of working men, led by two barristers, visited the area investigating a complaint that large landowners were keeping for their own sport of deer shooting, large areas of land which could be used to greater benefit for the people. Their report revealed that: 'The Atholl deer forest is of such a barren soil that it is totally unsuitable for small holdings, allotments, pendicles or crofts. The reason for this is that it consists of moss, peat, boulders and swamps. There is no way it could be used for agricultural purposes, rather its use as a deer forest increased employment or   unities.'

I will end this chapter and the book,   a poem told me by my great friend the late Mr Alec Mack..c, with whom I have spent many enlightening hours up the Glen:

> As the last vale to be exalted,
> As the last hill to be made low,
> Out of thy loving kindness Lord,
> Leave us Glen Tilt and Beinn a' Ghlo.

Glossary

Allenarlie	Only.
Astricted	Legally bound to a mill by thirlage.
Augmentation	Increase in the amount of a periodical payment such as stipend or rent.
Baron Bailie	A magistrate appointed by the lord-superior. Estate created by direct grant from the
Barony	Estate created by direct grant from the Crown, constituting a freehold barony.
Beiting	Mending, by making additions.
Bere	A coarse form of barley, once widely grown in Scotland.
Biggings	Buildings.
Boll	A volumetric grain measurement, a boll of oatmeal weighing approximately 140 lb.
Bonnet-laird	One who farmed land in its natural state, as a tenant, at a nominal rent for a long lease.
Bowman	Tenant of a cattle farm.
Calsay	Old spelling of causey, a road laid with cobble-stones.
Carriage	Service demanded from tenants which could be a long or short carriage.
Cast peat	Dig and cut peat.
Casualties	Payment of rent in kind, e.g. a quart of butter.
Change-house	Place where horses were changed, which developed into an inn.
Charter	A deed granted by a superior for land.
Coble	Patch up or mend coarsely.
Conversion	Cash equivalent of rent in kind.
Cooper	One who makes barrels, casks.
Cottar	Holder of a small piece of land, held in return for services, often labouring.
Croy	A mound or quay projecting into a river to break the force of the stream.

Crue lamb	Lamb kept in a pen.
Darg	A day's work.
Davoch	A unit of land measurement describing arable ground, townships and their grazing capacity.
Dinmont	Male sheep between first and second shearing.
Disposition	A deed for the transfer of property.
Door snaik	Door latch.
Drover	Person who drives sheep and cattle to market.
Dyke	A dry stone or turf wall to enclose a field, or mark a boundary.
Ell	A measurement of length, the Scottish ell being about 37 inches.
Fank	A stone enclosure for sheep.
Fencibles	Local Militia.
Feu	The buyer held land provided he built on it and paid rent, or feu duty. He was virtually the owner as long as he observed certain conditions.
Feuar	One who takes land in feu.
Fir	Bogwood used for candles.
Firlot	Unit of volume, equal to ¼ of a boll.
Furlong	Unit of measurement, equal to ⅛ of a mile.
Gimmer	One to two year old ewe.
Grindable cornes	Oats and barley grown within the thirl for household use.
Hained	Grassland preserved for hay.
Harling	Roughcasting a wall.
Haugh	Level ground near a river.
Head dyke	Wall to separate arable and meadow ground from hill pasture.
Heifer	A young cow.
Hogg	A yearling sheep not yet shorn.
Kill	A kiln for drying corn or burning lime.
Kindly tenant	A holder of land who, without a charter, came to have a sort of hereditary right, usually constituted by entry in a landowner's rent book.

Knaveship	A small proportion of grain ground at a mill which was the perquisite of the under-miller or miller's servant.
Lade	Channel leading water from the river or dam to the water wheel.
Law burrows	A process whereby a court can protect someone who believes he is in danger, by ordering another not to molest him.
Lazy-bed	A bed for growing potatoes, the seed being covered with earth dug out of trenches along both sides.
Lead peat	Cart peat from the moss.
Lint	Flax, used for making linen.
Marl	Limy clay used as manure.
Mart cow	Cow, fattened, killed and salted for winter use.
Merk	A silver coin worth 13/4d Scots.
Merkland	Term used for assessing land, which gave employment to one plough and one family in the arable parts. It was divisible into such fractions as ten shilling land (¾ merk), forty shilling land (3 merks).
Mortified	Given as a charitable bequest.
Moss	A boggy place where peat was dug.
Multure	Duty, consisting of a proportion of the grain ground, exacted by the proprietor of a mill on all corn ground.
Pean	Pane of glass.
Peck	Unit of volume, equal to ¼ firlot.
Pendicle	Small portion of land allotted by the farmer to his labourers and servants.
Plenishing	Furnishing a house.
Plenshons	Nails.
Ploughland	A unit of land, the exact extent being variable.
Poind	To impound.
Poindler	A herd who prevented straying animals from moving on to the shieling.
Quey	A heifer.
Ribbes	Bars of a grate.

Rood	Approximately 18 feet (six ells).
Ret	To steep flax in a lint pool, separating the woody core from the fibre.
Roup	Sale by auction.
Run-rig	Land where the alternate ridges of a field were worked by different tenants.
Stane	Stone.
Scots £	Worth a twelfth of a pound Sterling. By 1750 it was rapidly being phased out.
Sequestration	To take livestock, implements and furniture on leased premises to satisfy a claim for rent.
Services	A method of paying rent e.g. delivering a load of coal to the landlord's house.
Servitude of pasturage	A burden on a piece of land whereby the proprietor is restrained from the full use of what is his own.
Shieling	Grazing ground and bothies used in summer.
Shillen bands	Door hinges.
Sit-house	Dwelling-house, as distinct from a house used for any other purpose.
Spriggs	Small headless nails.
Stipend	Remuneration of a parish minister.
Stirk	Young cattle beast between one and two years old.
Stot	Bullock between two and three years old.
Straitened	Distressed, restricted.
Subset	Sublet.
Tabills	Tables.
Tack	A lease.
Thanage	A tenure of land in return for personal service, held directly by the King.
Thane	Supporter of the Scottish monarchy who was granted land.
Thirlage	The system whereby tenants cultivating certain lands were obliged to take their corn to a particular mill for grinding.
Tipling house	Ale house, tavern.
Topmaster	(Topsman) who assisted drovers by riding ahead to arrange a stance for the night and generally planned the route.

Transhumance	The movement of animals from the fields near the township to rough grazings some distance away.
Tups	Rams.
Wadsett	A pledge of land in security but with a right of recovery on payment to the wadsetter (the creditor).
Warrant	A written authority from a court authorising certain actions such as a search of premises or an eviction.
Wedder	(Wether), a castrated male sheep.
Win peat	Stack peat to dry.
Yeld cattle	Cows not in milk.

Sources and Bibliography

1. Manuscript Sources

British Library, London
  Roy's Military Survey of Scotland, 1747-1755
  Wade Manuscripts

Charter Room, Blair Castle
  Charters, rentals, manuscripts, letters, maps and plans

Clan Donnachaidh Museum, Falls of Bruar
  Writings of General Robertson circa 1790
  Rolls of persons in full communion, Blair Estate population, 1909
  Tales of Toll-bars and Toll-roads by James Robertson of Rannoch

General Register Office for Scotland, Edinburgh
  Parochial Registers for Parishes of Blair Atholl and Kingussie
  Census of Population for Parishes of Blair Atholl and Kingussie, 1841-1891

King's College Library, Aberdeen University
  List of tenants in the Brae Lands, 1778
  Population below Strowan and Blair, 1823

National Library of Scotland, Edinburgh
  Wade Manuscripts
  Pont Manuscripts

Sandeman Library, Perth
  Minutes of Highway Committee, 1765-1839
  Minutes of Atholl Turnpike Road Trustees

Post Office Records, London

Scottish Record Office, Edinburgh
  Gordon of Huntly Papers

Robertson of Lude Papers
Tummel Bridge Contract

2. Places of Reference
British Library, State Papers Room, London

Central Reference Library, Edinburgh

Ordnance Survey, Archaeological Department, Edinburgh

School of Scottish Studies, Edinburgh University

Scottish Horse Museum, Dunkeld

Society of Antiquaries of Scotland, Edinburgh

3. Parliamentary and State Papers
Reports of Commission for making Roads and Bridges in the Highlands:
> 1st Report 1804; 3rd Report 1807; 5th Report 1819; 8th Report 1822; 9th Report 1823; 10th Report 1824; 14th Report 1828; 15th Report 1829; 23rd Report 1837

4. Maps and Plans

1600	Timothy Pont	*Mapp of Garry and its Branches.*
1600	Timothy Pont	*Journey through Atholl and Renna.*
1654	Johan Blaeu	*Atlas Novus: Braid-Allaban, Atholia, Marrai Superior, Badenocha, Strath-Spea, Lochabria.*
1689	Rob Greene	*A new map of Scotland with the Roads.*
1718	Herman Moll	*A pocket companion of ye roads of ye north part of Great Britain called Scotland.*
1719	Board of Ordnance	*A plan of the Barracks at Ruthven in Badenoch.*
1725	Herman Moll	*The Roads between Innersnait, Ruthven of Badenoch, Kiliwhiman and Fort William in the Highlands of North Britain.*
1742	R. Cooper	*A map of His Majesty's Roads from Edinburgh to Inverness . . ..*
1745	Will. Edgar	*A new and correct map of Perthshire.*

1745	Thomas Willdey	*A map of the King's Roads, made by His Excellency General Wade, in the Highlands of Scotland.*
1747-1755	William Roy	*Military Survey of Scotland.*
1756	John Lesslie	*A topographical map of Loch Rannoch.*
1767	John Lesslie	*Contraverted March betwixt annexed Estates of Loch Garry in Perthshire and His Grace Duke of Gordon's estates in Badenoch, Inverness-shire.*
1770	Alex Taylor	*Plan of contraverted ground in Drumochter between Duke of Gordon's Estate of Badenoch, Sir Robert Menzies' estate of Rannoch and annexed estate of Loch Garry.*
1771	William Tennoch	*Part of Annexed estate of Loch Garry in Atholl.*
1773	William Tennoch	*Plan of the high hill grazings of Loch Garry in Atholl.*

5. Maps and Plans from Blair Castle Collection

1725	Herman Moll	*The North part of Perthshire containing Atholl and Broadalbin (from a set of thirty six new and correct maps of Scotland).*
1744	John Tinney	*Plan of the Castle Gardens, Plantations.*
1744	Chas. Esplen	*A plan for Blair in Atholl.*
1750	James Dorret	*A general map of Scotland and Islands.*
1758	James Dorret	*Plan of Atholl House Gardens, Parks and Inclosures.*
1780	James Stobie	*Plan of Blair in Atholl, Forests of Tarff, Benechrombie in Perthshire.*
1780	James Stobie	*Plan of lands in Strathtumble.*
c.1780	James Stobie	*Upper Glen Garry.*
1783	James Stobie	*Counties of Perth and Clackmannan.*
1784	James Stobie	*Plan of North East Quarter of Perthshire.*
1790		*Draught of the Barony and Lands of Lude as presently possessed to the south and east of the Water of Tilt.*
c.1790	James Stobie	*Detailed plans of Brae Lands settlements.*
1805	James Stobie	*The Counties of Perth and Clackmannan.*

1807	Aaron Arrowsmith	*Map of Scotland constructed from Original materials obtained under the authority of the Parliamentary Commissioners ....*
1808	David Buist	*Plan of the Commonty lying betwixt Glens of Fender and Tilt belonging to the Duke of Atholl and James Robertson Esq: of Lude.*
1815	J. Stirton	*North East Quarter of Perthshire by Mr Stobie, copied.*
1821	J. Douglas	*North West Perthshire.*
1821	J. Douglas	*Outline Plan of Lands of Bohespike and Strathtummel.*
1823		*Estate map of Atholl Forest.*
1826		*Plan of Blairuachter.*
1826		*Plan of Woodend, Coult, Urrard.*
1828	Joseph Mitchell	*Sketch of the present Highland Road between Inverness and Perth, showing also proposed alterations.*
c.1830		*Plan of Glen Tilt showing Right of Way.*
1830		*Plan Book of Blair District.*
1836		*Atholl Deer Forest.*
1846		*Sketch of Glen Bruar Shooting Ground.*
1860-1867		*Ordnance Survey First Edition 6"/mile.*
1900		*Ordnance Survey Second Edition 6"/mile.*

6. Publications

Adams. I.H.	1976	*Agrarian landscape terms: a glossary for historical geography.*
Anderson, George and Peter	1843	*Guide to the Highlands and Islands of Scotland.*
Atholl, John, 7th Duke	1908	*Chronicles of the Atholl and Tullibardine Families.*
Barron, James	1903	*Newspaper index and annals – The Northern Highlands in the 19th Century: volume 1.*
Bowstead, Christopher	1915	*Facts and Fancies about Kilmaveonaig.*

Bruce, Robert   1932   *The Great North Road over the Grampians: Minutes of Proceedings of Institution of Civil Engineers.*

Burt   1974   *Letters from the North of Scotland: volumes 1 and 2.*

Cairngorm Club Journal   1911   *volume VII, 1913 volume IX.*

Celtic Review   1908/1909

Chambers, Robert   1891   *Domestic Annals of Scotland.*

Chambers   1982   *Scots Dictionary.*

Chambers   1971   *20th Century Dictionary.*

Coles, Fred.   1907/08   *Report on stone circles surveyed in Perthshire: Proceedings of Society of Antiquaries, volume XLII.*

Defoe, Daniel   1769   *A Tour through the whole of Great Britain.*

Duff, David   1968   *Victoria in the Highlands.*

Duncan, A.G.M.   1982   *Students' glossary of Scottish Legal Terms.*

Dwelly, Edward   1967   *Illustrated Gaelic to English Dictionary.*

Fergusson, Charles   1877/78   *Gaelic Names of Trees and Shrubs: Transactions of the Gaelic Society of Inverness, volume VII.*

Garnett, T.   1811   *Observations on a Tour through the Highlands and part of the Western Isles of Scotland.*

Grant, Elizabeth   1898   *Memoirs of a Highland Lady.*

Helps, Arthur (ed.)   1868   *Leaves from the Journal of our Life in the Highlands.*

Heron, Robert   1793   *Observations made in a Journey through the Western Counties of Scotland: volume I.*

Hume-Brown, P.   1884   *Early Travellers in Scotland.*

Kerr, John   *Transactions of the Gaelic Society of Inverness.*

     1975   *Old Grampian Highways, Volume XLIX.*

	1984	*Wade in Atholl, Volume LIII.*
	1987	*East by Tilt, Volume LIV.*
Larkin, William	1818	*Sketches of a Tour in the Highlands of Scotland.*
MacCulloch, John	1816	*A Geological Description of Glen Tilt: Transactions of the Geological Society, volume 3.*
MacFarlane's	1906	*Geographical Collections.*
MacGibbon, David and Ross	1897	*The Ecclesiastical Architecture of Scotland: volume 3.*
Mackenzie, Sir Kenneth	1897	*General Wade and his Roads: Inverness Scientific Society and Field Club Transactions, volume 5.*
Mackintosh, Charles	1875	*Invernessiana.*
Mackintosh, Lauchlan	1828, 1829, 1836	*Extracts from the Inverness Journal*
Macpherson, Malcolm	1965	*Legends of Badenoch.*
Marshall, William	1880	*Historic Scenes of Perthshire.*
Miller. Ronald	1967	*Land use by Summer Shielings.*
Mitchell, Joseph	1884	*Reminiscences of my Life in the Highlands.*
Murray, Sarah	1799	*A Companion and useful Guide to the Beauties of Scotland.*
New Statistical Account	1845	*Parish of Blair Atholl.*
Pennant, Thomas	1774	*A Tour of Scotland 1769.*
Pococke, Richard	1887	*Tours in Scotland 1747, 1750, 1760.*
Rickman, John	1838	*Life of Thomas Telford, Civil Engineer.*
Robertson, J.A.	1860	*Comitatus de Atholia. The Earldom of Atholl, its boundaries stated.*
Royal Scottish Geographical Society	1973	*The Early Maps of Scotland: volume 1.*
	1983	*volume 2.*
Salmond, J.B.	1934	*Wade in Scotland.*
Scots Magazine	1746	*May, June, 1754 November.*
Scottish Mountaineering Club Guide	1931	*The Cairngorms.*

	1941	*Scottish National Dictionary.*
Scrope, William	1838	*Art of Deer Stalking.*
Shaw, John	1984	*Water Power in Scotland.*
Sinton, Thomas		*Poetry of Badenoch.*
Statistical Account	1792	*Parishes of Blair Atholl and Kingussie.*
Suiton, James		*Notes on the Rev. Francis Gastrell's Tour through Scotland in 1760.*
Watson, W.J.	1926	*History of the Celtic Place Names of Scotland.*
Wishart, Rev. George	1893	*James, First Marquis of Montrose.*
Wordsworth, Dorothy	1874	*Recollections of a Tour made in Scotland A.D. 1803.*

Index